ONE WEEK LOAN

Cram101 Textbook Outlines to accompany:

The Development of Children

Cole, Cole, Lightfoot, 5th Edition

An Academic Internet Publishers (AIPI) publication (c) 2007.

You have a discounted membership at www.Cram101.com with this book.

Get all of the practice tests for the chapters of this textbook, and access in-depth reference material for writing essays and papers. Here is an example from a Cram101 Biology text:

When you need problem solving help with math, stats, and other disciplines, www.Cram101.com will walk through the formulas and solutions step by step.

With Cram101.com online, you also have access to extensive reference material.

You will nail those essays and papers. Here is an example from a Cram101 Biology text:

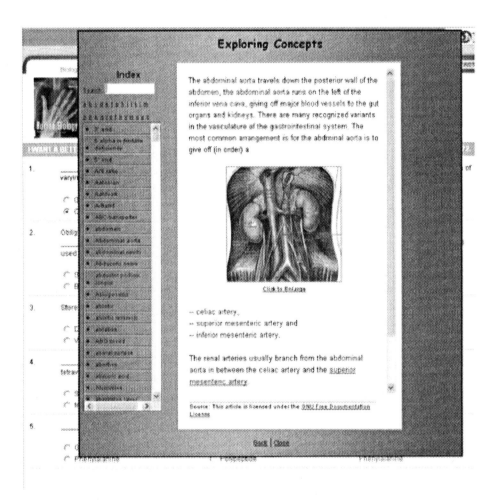

Visit **www.Cram101.com**, click Sign Up at the top of the screen, and enter DK73DW3635 in the promo code box on the registration screen. Access to www.Cram101.com is normally $9.95, but because you have purchased this book, your access fee is only $4.95. Sign up and stop highlighting textbooks forever.

Learning System

Cram101 Textbook Outlines is a learning system. The notes in this book are the highlights of your textbook, you will never have to highlight a book again.

How to use this book. Take this book to class, it is your notebook for the lecture. The notes and highlights on the left hand side of the pages follow the outline and order of the textbook. All you have to do is follow along while your intructor presents the lecture. Circle the items emphasized in class and add other important information on the right side. With Cram101 Textbook Outlines you'll spend less time writing and more time listening. Learning becomes more efficient.

Cram101.com Online

Increase your studying efficiency by using Cram101.com's practice tests and online reference material. It is the perfect complement to Cram101 Textbook Outlines. Use self-teaching matching tests or simulate in-class testing with comprehensive multiple choice tests, or simply use Cram's true and false tests for quick review. Cram101.com even allows you to enter your in-class notes for an integrated studying format combining the textbook notes with your class notes.

Visit **www.Cram101.com**, click Sign Up at the top of the screen, and enter **DK73DW3635** in the promo code box on the registration screen. Access to www.Cram101.com is normally $9.95, but because you have purchased this book, your access fee is only $4.95. Sign up and stop highlighting textbooks forever.

The Development of Children
Cole, Cole, Lightfoot, 5th

CONTENTS

Early childhood	Early childhood refers to the developmental period extending from the end of infancy to about 5 or 6 years of age; sometimes called the preschool years.
Sensation	Sensation is the first stage in the chain of biochemical and neurologic events that begins with the impinging of a stimulus upon the receptor cells of a sensory organ, which then leads to perception, the mental state that is reflected in statements like "I see a uniformly blue wall."
Society	The social sciences use the term society to mean a group of people that form a semi-closed (or semi-open) social system, in which most interactions are with other individuals belonging to the group.
Human nature	Human nature is the fundamental nature and substance of humans, as well as the range of human behavior that is believed to be invariant over long periods of time and across very different cultural contexts.
Social isolation	Social isolation refers to a type of loneliness that occurs when a person lacks a sense of integrated involvement. Being deprived of participation in a group or community involving companionship, shared interests, organized activities, and meaningful roles causes a person to feel alone.
Hartup	According to Hartup, the single best childhood predictor of adult adaptation is not school grades, and not classroom behavior, but rather, the adequacy with which the child gets along with other children.
Child development	Scientific study of the processes of change from conception through adolescence is called child development.
Stages	Stages represent relatively discrete periods of time in which functioning is qualitatively different from functioning at other periods.
Theories	Theories are logically self-consistent models or frameworks describing the behavior of a certain natural or social phenomenon. They are broad explanations and predictions concerning phenomena of interest.
Scientific method	Psychologists gather data in order to describe, understand, predict, and control behavior. Scientific method refers to an approach that can be used to discover accurate information. It includes these steps: understand the problem, collect data, draw conclusions, and revise research conclusions.
Locke	In 1690, Locke wrote his Essay Concerning Human Understanding. The essay arugued for empiricism, that ideas come only from experience. In other words, there are no innate ideas. The tabula rasa or blank slate was his metaphor.
Shaping	The concept of reinforcing successive, increasingly accurate approximations to a target behavior is called shaping. The target behavior is broken down into a hierarchy of elemental steps, each step more sophisticated then the last. By successively reinforcing each of the the elemental steps, a form of differential reinforcement, until that step is learned while extinguishing the step below, the target behavior is gradually achieved.
Temperament	Temperament refers to a basic, innate disposition to change behavior. The activity level is an important dimension of temperament.
Rousseau	Rousseau rejected the idea of the blank slate. He believed that learning was a natural consequence of human existence. Further, he thought socialization unimportant in development. Because of his insistence that childhood was different than adulthood and his creation of stages of development, he is known as the father of developmental psychology.
Affect	A subjective feeling or emotional tone often accompanied by bodily expressions noticeable to others is called affect.
Species	Species refers to a reproductively isolated breeding population.
Darwin	Darwin achieved lasting fame as originator of the theory of evolution through natural selection. His book Expression of Emotions in Man and Animals is generally considered the first text on comparative psychology.

Go to **Cram101.com** for the Practice Tests for this Chapter.

Origin of Species	The Origin of Species by Charles Darwin makes the argument that groups of organisms gradually evolve through the process of natural selection. Characteristics that favor survival and reproduction are passed on to the next generation, those that do not, are gradually lost.
Motives	Needs or desires that energize and direct behavior toward a goal are motives.
Brain	The brain controls and coordinates most movement, behavior and homeostatic body functions such as heartbeat, blood pressure, fluid balance and body temperature. Functions of the brain are responsible for cognition, emotion, memory, motor learning and other sorts of learning. The brain is primarily made up of two types of cells: glia and neurons.
Attention	Attention is the cognitive process of selectively concentrating on one thing while ignoring other things. Psychologists have labeled three types of attention: sustained attention, selective attention, and divided attention.
Neuron	The neuron is the primary cell of the nervous system. They are found in the brain, the spinal cord, in the nerves and ganglia of the peripheral nervous system. It is a specialized cell that conducts impulses through the nervous system and contains three major parts: cell body, dendrites, and an axon. It can have many dendrites but only one axon.
Insight	Insight refers to a sudden awareness of the relationships among various elements that had previously appeared to be independent of one another.
Evolution	Commonly used to refer to gradual change, evolution is the change in the frequency of alleles within a population from one generation to the next. This change may be caused by different mechanisms, including natural selection, genetic drift, or changes in population (gene flow).
Descartes	Descartes was concerned with the sharp contrast between the certainty of mathematics and the controversial nature of philosophy, and came to believe that the sciences could be made to yield results as certain as those of mathematics. He introduced the method of rationalism for arriving at knowledge. He also saw the human condition as a competition between the body and soul, introducing the concept of dualism.
Continuity of species	The continuity of species refers to the theory that all living organisms are adaptations of earlier life forms and are genetically related.
Quantitative	A quantitative property is one that exists in a range of magnitudes, and can therefore be measured. Measurements of any particular quantitative property are expressed as as a specific quantity, referred to as a unit, multiplied by a number.
Quantitative change	Quantitative change refers to change in number or amount, such as in height, weight, or size of vocabulary.
Qualitative change	A qualitative change refers to a change in kind, structure, or organization, such as the change from nonverbal to verbal communication.
Babbling	Babbling is a stage in child language acquisition, during which an infant appears to be experimenting with making the sounds of language, but not yet producing any recognizable words.
Discontinuity view	The discontinuity view emphasizes change and growth in relationships over time. As people grow up, they develop many different types of relationships. Each of these relationships is structurally different. With each new type of relationship, individuals encounter new modes of relating.
Attachment	Attachment is the tendency to seek closeness to another person and feel secure when that person is present.
Continuity view	A developmental view that emphasizes the role of early parent-child relationships in constructing the child's way of relating to people throughout the life span is the continuity view.
Infancy	The developmental period that extends from birth to 18 or 24 months is called infancy.

Go to **Cram101.com** for the Practice Tests for this Chapter.

Stage theory	Stage theory characterizes development by hypothesizing the existence of distinct, and often critical, periods of life. Each period follows one another in an orderly sequence.
Construct	A generalized concept, such as anxiety or gravity, is a construct.
Continuity Theory	Continuity Theory states for behavior based on a disorderly perceptual process, subjects learn simultaneously about all the stimuli that are present and then respond when stimuli resemble any from the original training session.
Acute	Acute means sudden, sharp, and abrupt. Usually short in duration.
Cognitive development	The process by which a child's understanding of the world changes as a function of age and experience is called cognitive development.
Biological predisposition	The genetic readiness of animals and humans to perform certain behaviors is a biological predisposition.
Predisposition	Predisposition refers to an inclination or diathesis to respond in a certain way, either inborn or acquired. In abnormal psychology, it is a factor that lowers the ability to withstand stress and inclines the individual toward pathology.
Nurture	Nurture refers to the environmental influences on behavior due to nutrition, culture, socioeconomic status, and learning.
Plasticity	The capacity for modification and change is referred to as plasticity.
Critical period	A period of time when an innate response can be elicited by a particular stimulus is referred to as the critical period.
Sensitive period	A sensitive period is a developmental window in which a predisposed behavior is most likely to develop given appropriate stimulation. In linguistic theory, the period from about 18 months to puberty is when the brain is thought to be primed for learning language because of plasticity of the brain.
Individual differences	Individual differences psychology studies the ways in which individual people differ in their behavior. This is distinguished from other aspects of psychology in that although psychology is ostensibly a study of individuals, modern psychologists invariably study groups.
Identical twins	Identical twins occur when a single egg is fertilized to form one zygote (monozygotic) but the zygote then divides into two separate embryos. The two embryos develop into foetuses sharing the same womb. Monozygotic twins are genetically identical unless there has been a mutation in development, and they are almost always the same gender.
Innate	Innate behavior is not learned or influenced by the environment, rather, it is present or predisposed at birth.
Metabolism	Metabolism is the biochemical modification of chemical compounds in living organisms and cells.
Trait	An enduring personality characteristic that tends to lead to certain behaviors is called a trait. The term trait also means a genetically inherited feature of an organism.
Adolescence	The period of life bounded by puberty and the assumption of adult responsibilities is adolescence.
Basic research	Basic research has as its primary objective the advancement of knowledge and the theoretical understanding of the relations among variables . It is exploratory and often driven by the researcher's curiosity, interest or hunch.
Applied research	Applied research is done to solve specific, practical questions; its primary aim is not to gain knowledge for its own sake. It can be exploratory but often it is descriptive. It is almost always done on the basis of basic research.
Learning	Learning is a relatively permanent change in behavior that results from experience. Thus, to attribute a behavioral change to learning, the change must be relatively permanent and must result from

experience.

Attitude	An enduring mental representation of a person, place, or thing that evokes an emotional response and related behavior is called attitude.
Action research	Originally formulated by social psychologist Kurt Lewin, action research is a disciplined method for intentional learning from experience
Reflection	Reflection is the process of rephrasing or repeating thoughts and feelings expressed, making the person more aware of what they are saying or thinking.
Reliability	Reliability means the extent to which a test produces a consistent , reproducible score .
Validity	The extent to which a test measures what it is intended to measure is called validity.
Scientific research	Research that is objective, systematic, and testable is called scientific research.
Naturalistic observation	Naturalistic observation is a method of observation that involves observing subjects in their natural habitats. Researchers take great care in avoiding making interferences with the behavior they are observing by using unobtrusive methods.
Ethology	Where comparative psychology sees the study of animal behavior in the context of what is known about human psychology, ethology sees the study of animal behavior in the context of what is known about animal anatomy and physiology.
Ethnography	Ethnography is a holistic research method founded in the idea that a system's properties cannot necessarily be accurately understood independently of each other.
Ecology	Ecology refers to the branch of biology that deals with the relationships between living organisms and their environment.
Population	Population refers to all members of a well-defined group of organisms, events, or things.
Bronfenbrenner	Bronfenbrenner was a co-founder of the U.S. national Head Start program and founder of the Ecological Theory of Development.
Roger Barker	In his classic work "Ecological Psychology" (1968), Roger Barker argued that human behavior was radically situated: in other words, you couldn't make predictions about human behavior unless you know what situation or context or environment the human in question was in.
Scheme	According to Piaget, a hypothetical mental structure that permits the classification and organization of new information is called a scheme.
Hypothesis	A specific statement about behavior or mental processes that is testable through research is a hypothesis.
Experimental group	Experimental group refers to any group receiving a treatment effect in an experiment.
Low birth weight	Low birth weight is a fetus that weighs less than 2500 g (5 lb 8 oz) regardless of gestational age.
Experimental manipulation	The change that an experimenter deliberately produces in a situation under study is called the experimental manipulation.
Control group	A group that does not receive the treatment effect in an experiment is referred to as the control group or sometimes as the comparison group.
Laboratory setting	Research setting in which the behavior of interest does not naturally occur is called a laboratory setting.
Correlation	A statistical technique for determining the degree of association between two or more variables is referred to as correlation.

Go to **Cram101.com** for the Practice Tests for this Chapter.

Causation	Causation concerns the time order relationship between two or more objects such that if a specific antecedent condition occurs the same consequent must always follow.
Correlation coefficient	Correlation coefficient refers to a number from +1.00 to -1.00 that expresses the direction and extent of the relationship between two variables. The closer to 1, the stronger the relationship. The sign, + or -, indicates the direction.
Positive correlation	A relationship between two variables in which both vary in the same direction is called a positive correlation.
Negative correlation	A negative correlation refers to a relationship between two variables in which one variable increases as the other decreases.
Psychological test	Psychological test refers to a standardized measure of a sample of a person's behavior.
Intelligence test	An intelligence test is a standardized means of assessing a person's current mental ability, for example, the Stanford-Binet test and the Wechsler Adult Intelligence Scale.
Clinical method	Studying psychological problems and therapies in clinical settings is referred to as the clinical method. It usually involves case histories, pathology, or non-experimentally controlled environments.
Research method	The scope of the research method is to produce some new knowledge. This, in principle, can take three main forms: Exploratory research; Constructive research; and Empirical research.
Strange situation	An observational measure of infant attachment that requires the infant to move through a series of introductions, separations, and reunions with the caregiver and an adult stranger in a prescribed order is called Ainsworth's strange situation.
Piaget	Piaget argued that young children's answers were qualitatively different than older children rather than quantitative. There are two major aspects to his theory: the process of coming to know and the stages we move through as we gradually acquire this ability.
Social class	Social class describes the relationships between people in hierarchical societies or cultures. Those with more power usually subordinate those with less power.
Research design	A research design tests a hypothesis. The basic typess are: descriptive, correlational, and experimental.
Longitudinal design	A research design in which investigators observe one group of subjects repeatedly over a period of time is called a longitudinal design.
Developmental psychology	The branch of psychology that studies the patterns of growth and change occurring throughout life is referred to as developmental psychology.
Microgenetic	A design that allows researchers to directly observe change by repeated testing over a relatively short time period is called a microgenetic study. The idea is to study change as change is occurring.
Anatomy	Anatomy is the branch of biology that deals with the structure and organization of living things. It can be divided into animal anatomy (zootomy) and plant anatomy (phytonomy). Major branches of anatomy include comparative anatomy, histology, and human anatomy.
Attention deficit hyperactivity disorder	A learning disability marked by inattention, impulsiveness, a low tolerance for frustration, and a great deal of inappropriate activity is the attention deficit hyperactivity disorder.
Hyperactivity	Hyperactivity can be described as a state in which a individual is abnormally easily excitable and exuberant. Strong emotional reactions and a very short span of attention is also typical for the individual.
Psychosis	Psychosis is a generic term for mental states in which the components of rational thought and

perception are severely impaired. Persons experiencing a psychosis may experience hallucinations, hold paranoid or delusional beliefs, demonstrate personality changes and exhibit disorganized thinking. This is usually accompanied by features such as a lack of insight into the unusual or bizarre nature of their behavior, difficulties with social interaction and impairments in carrying out the activities of daily living.

Cerebral cortex	The cerebral cortex is the outermost layer of the cerebrum and has a grey color. It is made up of four lobes and it is involved in many complex brain functions including memory, perceptual awareness, "thinking", language and consciousness. The cerebral cortex receives sensory information from many different sensory organs eg: eyes, ears, etc. and processes the information.
Longitudinal research	Research that studies the same subjects over an extended period of time, usually several years or more, is called longitudinal research.
Ethnic group	An ethnic group is a culture or subculture whose members are readily distinguishable by outsiders based on traits originating from a common racial, national, linguistic, or religious source. Members of an ethnic group are often presumed to be culturally or biologically similar, although this is not in fact necessarily the case.
Longitudinal study	Longitudinal study is a type of developmental study in which the same group of participants is followed and measured for an extended period of time, often years.
Biased sample	A biased sample is one that is falsely taken to be typical of a population from which it is drawn.
Cohort	A cohort is a group of individuals defined by their date of birth.
Sequential design	A combination of the cross-sectional and longitudinal research methods that involves a repeated study of different cohorts over an extended period of time is a sequential design.
Longitudinal approach	The Longitudinal approach is a research strategy in which the same individuals are studied over a period of time, usually several years or more.
Representative sample	Representative sample refers to a sample of participants selected from the larger population in such a way that important subgroups within the population are included in the sample in the same proportions as they are found in the larger population.
Threshold	In general, a threshold is a fixed location or value where an abrupt change is observed. In the sensory modalities, it is the minimum amount of stimulus energy necessary to elicit a sensory response.
Vygotsky	The Vygotsky model of human development has been termed as a sociocultural approach. The individual's development is a result of his or her culture.
Analogy	An analogy is a comparison between two different things, in order to highlight some form of similarity. Analogy is the cognitive process of transferring information from a particular subject to another particular subject.
Watson	Watson, the father of behaviorism, developed the term "Behaviorism" as a name for his proposal to revolutionize the study of human psychology in order to put it on a firm experimental footing.
Informed consent	The term used by psychologists to indicate that a person has agreed to participate in research after receiving information about the purposes of the study and the nature of the treatments is informed consent. Even with informed consent, subjects may withdraw from any experiment at any time.
Developmental psychologist	A psychologist interested in human growth and development from conception until death is referred to as a developmental psychologist.
Maturation	The orderly unfolding of traits, as regulated by the genetic code is called maturation.
Arnold Gesell	Arnold Gesell was a pioneer in the field of child development and developmental measurement. He constructed the Gesell dome, a one-way mirror shaped as a dome, under which children could be observed without being disturbed.

Sigmund Freud	Sigmund Freud was the founder of the psychoanalytic school, based on his theory that unconscious motives control much behavior, that particular kinds of unconscious thoughts and memories are the source of neurosis, and that neurosis could be treated through bringing these unconscious thoughts and memories to consciousness in psychoanalytic treatment.
Personality	Personality refers to the pattern of enduring characteristics that differentiates a person, the patterns of behaviors that make each individual unique.
Psychodynamic	Most psychodynamic approaches are centered around the idea of a maladapted function developed early in life (usually childhood) which are at least in part unconscious. This maladapted function (a.k.a. defense mechanism) does not do well in place of a normal/healthy one.
Erik Erikson	Erik Erikson conceived eight stages of development, each confronting the individual with its own psychosocial demands, that continued into old age. Personality development, according to Erikson, takes place through a series of crises that must be overcome and internalized by the individual in preparation for the next developmental stage. Such crisis are not catastrophes but vulnerabilities.
Resurgence	Resurgence refers to the reappearance during extinction, of a previously reinforced behavior.
Exogenous	Exogenous refers to an action or object coming from outside a system.
Adaptation	Adaptation is a lowering of sensitivity to a stimulus following prolonged exposure to that stimulus. Behavioral adaptations are special ways a particular organism behaves to survive in its natural habitat.
Necessary condition	A circumstance required for a particular phenomenon to occur is a necessary condition if and only if the condition does not occur in the absense of the circumstance.
Ego	In Freud's view the Ego serves to balance our primitive needs and our moral beliefs and taboos. Relying on experience, a healthy Ego provides the ability to adapt to reality and interact with the outside world.
Infantile sexuality	Freud's insistence that sexuality does not begin with adolescence, that babies are sexual too, is referred to as infantile sexuality.
Puberty	Puberty refers to the process of physical changes by which a child's body becomes an adult body capable of reproduction.
Intimacy versus isolation	The life crisis of young adulthood, which is characterized by the task of developing binding intimate relationships is referred to as Erikson's intimacy versus isolation stage.
Generativity versus stagnation	Generativity versus stagnation is Erikson's term for the crisis of middle adulthood. The individual is characterized by the task of being productive and contributing to younger generations.
Generativity	Generativity refers to an adult's concern for and commitment to the well-being of future generations.
Integrity versus despair	Erikson's eighth and final stage of development is Integrity Versus Despair. In late adulthood individuals reflect on the past and either piece together a positive review or conclude that one's life has not been well spent.
Autonomy versus shame and doubt	In Erikson's second stage of development, autonomy versus shame and doubt, which occurs in late infancy and toddlerhood, infants begin to discover that their behavior is their own.
Early adulthood	The developmental period beginning in the late teens or early twenties and lasting into the thirties is called early adulthood; characterized by an increasing self-awareness.
Autonomy	Autonomy is the condition of something that does not depend on anything else.
Initiative versus guilt	Initiative versus guilt is Erikson's third stage of development, which occurs during the preschool years. As preschool children encounter a widening social world, they are challenged more than they were as infants.

Go to **Cram101.com** for the Practice Tests for this Chapter.
And, **NEVER** highlight a book again!

Guilt	Guilt describes many concepts related to a negative emotion or condition caused by actions which are believed to be, morally wrong. According to Freud, the avoidance of guilt is the basis for moral behavior.
Industry versus inferiority	Erikson's fourth stage of development, industry versus inferiority, develops in the elementary school years. Initiative brings children into contact with a new experiences. They direct their energy toward mastering knowledge and intellectual skills.
Identity versus role confusion	Identity versus role confusion, Erikson's fifth psychosocial stage, shows adolescents needing to establish their own identity and to form values to live by. Failure at this stage can lead to an identity crisis.
Personal identity	The portion of the self-concept that pertains to the self as a distinct, separate individual is called personal identity.
Superego	Frued's third psychic structure, which functions as a moral guardian and sets forth high standards for behavior is the superego.
Variability	Statistically, variability refers to how much the scores in a distribution spread out, away from the mean.
Prototype	A concept of a category of objects or events that serves as a good example of the category is called a prototype.
Connectedness	Connectedness, according to Cooper, consists of two dimensions: mutuality and permeability. Connectedness involves processes that link the self to others, as seen in acknowledgment of, respect for, and responsiveness to others.
Retina	The retina is a thin layer of cells at the back of the eyeball. It is the part of the eye which converts light into nervous signals. The retina contains photoreceptor cells which receive the light; the resulting neural signals then undergo complex processing by other neurons of the retina, and are transformed into action potentials in retinal ganglion cells whose axons form the optic nerve.
Sensorimotor	The first of Piaget's stages is the Sensorimotor stage. This stage typically ranges from birth to 2 years. In this stage, children experience the world through their senses. During this stage, object permanence and stranger anxiety develop.
Formal reasoning	The type of reasoning in which the form of an argument, not its semantic content, is crucial is referred to as formal reasoning.
Reasoning	Reasoning is the act of using reason to derive a conclusion from certain premises. There are two main methods to reach a conclusion,deductive reasoning and inductive reasoning.
Gene	A gene is an ultramicroscopic area of the chromosome. It is the smallest physical unit of the DNA molecule that carries a piece of hereditary information.
Sexual reproduction	Sexual reproduction is a biological process by which organisms create descendants through the combination of genetic material taken randomly and independently from two different members of the species.

Genetic disorder	A genetic disorder is a disease caused by abnormal expression of one or more genes in a person causing a clinical phenotype.
Immune system	The most important function of the human immune system occurs at the cellular level of the blood and tissues. The lymphatic and blood circulation systems are highways for specialized white blood cells. These cells include B cells, T cells, natural killer cells, and macrophages. All function with the primary objective of recognizing, attacking and destroying bacteria, viruses, cancer cells, and all substances seen as foreign.
Syndrome	The term syndrome is the association of several clinically recognizable features, signs, symptoms, phenomena or characteristics which often occur together, so that the presence of one feature indicates the presence of the others.
Gene	A gene is an ultramicroscopic area of the chromosome. It is the smallest physical unit of the DNA molecule that carries a piece of hereditary information.
Learning	Learning is a relatively permanent change in behavior that results from experience. Thus, to attribute a behavioral change to learning, the change must be relatively permanent and must result from experience.
Learning disability	A learning disability exists when there is a significant discrepancy between one's ability and achievement.
Fetus	A fetus develops from the end of the 8th week of pregnancy (when the major structures have formed), until birth.
Evolution	Commonly used to refer to gradual change, evolution is the change in the frequency of alleles within a population from one generation to the next. This change may be caused by different mechanisms, including natural selection, genetic drift, or changes in population (gene flow).
Species	Species refers to a reproductively isolated breeding population.
Sexual reproduction	Sexual reproduction is a biological process by which organisms create descendants through the combination of genetic material taken randomly and independently from two different members of the species.
Genetic abnormality	Any abnormality in the genes, including missing genes, extra genes, or defective genes is called genetic abnormality.
Chromosome	The DNA which carries genetic information in biological cells is normally packaged in the form of one or more large macromolecules called a chromosome. Humans normally have 46.
Double helix	The double helix is the structure of DNA. Each of the two strands forms a helix, and the two helices are held together through hydrogen bonds, ionic forces, hydrophobic interactions, and van der Waals forces forming a double helix.
Deoxyribonuc-eic acid	Deoxyribonucleic acid contains the genetic instructions specifying the biological development of all cellular forms of life. It is often referred to as the molecule of heredity, as it is responsible for the genetic propagation of most inherited traits.
Protein	A protein is a complex, high-molecular-weight organic compound that consists of amino acids joined by peptide bonds. It is essential to the structure and function of all living cells and viruses. Many are enzymes or subunits of enzymes.
Coding	In senation, coding is the process by which information about the quality and quantity of a stimulus is preserved in the pattern of action potentials sent through sensory neurons to the central nervous system.
Fallopian tube	A tube through which the eggs travel from the ovaries to the uterus is a fallopian tube.
Ejaculation	Ejaculation is the process of ejecting semen from the penis, and is usually accompanied by

Go to **Cram101.com** for the Practice Tests for this Chapter.

	orgasm as a result of sexual stimulation.
Uterus	The uterus or womb is the major female reproductive organ. The main function of the uterus is to accept a fertilized ovum which becomes implanted into the endometrium, and derives nourishment from blood vessels which develop exclusively for this purpose.
Zygote	A zygote is a cell that is the result of fertilization. That is, two haploid cells—usually (but not always) a sperm cell from a male and an ovum from a female—merge into a single diploid cell called the zygote.
Ovum	Ovum is a female sex cell or gamete.
Mitosis	Mitosis is the process by which a cell separates its duplicated genome into two identical halves.
Meiosis	The process of cell doubling and separation of chromosomes in which each pair of chromosomes in a cell separates, with one member of each pair going into each gamete is called meiosis.
Monozygotic	Identical twins occur when a single egg is fertilized to form one zygote, calld monozygotic, but the zygote then divides into two separate embryos. The two embryos develop into foetuses sharing the same womb. Monozygotic twins are genetically identical unless there has been a mutation in development, and they are almost always the same gender.
Genotype	The genotype is the specific genetic makeup of an individual, usually in the form of DNA. It codes for the phenotype of that individual. Any given gene will usually cause an observable change in an organism, known as the phenotype.
Dizygotic	Fraternal twins (commonly known as "non-identical twins") usually occur when two fertilized eggs are implanted in the uterine wall at the same time. The two eggs form two zygotes, and these twins are therefore also known as dizygotic.
Cytoplasm	Cytoplasm is the colloidal, semi-fluid matter contained within the cell's plasma membrane, in which organelles are suspended. In contrast to the protoplasm, the cytoplasm does not include the cell nucleus, the interior of which is made up of nucleoplasm.
Identical twins	Identical twins occur when a single egg is fertilized to form one zygote (monozygotic) but the zygote then divides into two separate embryos. The two embryos develop into foetuses sharing the same womb. Monozygotic twins are genetically identical unless there has been a mutation in development, and they are almost always the same gender.
X chromosome	The sex chromosomes are one of the 23 pairs of human chromosomes. Each person normally has one pair of sex chromosomes in each cell. Females have two X chromosomes, while males have one X and one Y chromosome. The X chromosome carries hundreds of genes but few, if any, of these have anything to do directly with sex determination.
Y chromosome	The Y chromosome is one of the two sex chromosomes in humans and most other mammals. The sex chromosomes are one of the 23 pairs of human chromosomes. The Y chromosome contains the fewest genes of any of the chromosomes. It contains the genes that cause testis development, thus determining maleness. It is usually contributed by the father.
Phenotype	The phenotype of an individual organism is either its total physical appearance and constitution, or a specific manifestation of a trait, such as size or eye color, that varies between individuals. Phenotype is determined to some extent by genotype, or by the identity of the alleles that an individual carries at one or more positions on the chromosomes.
Mendel	Mendel is often called the "father of genetics" for his study of the inheritance of traits in pea plants. Mendel showed that there was particulate inheritance of traits according to his laws of inheritance.
Trait	An enduring personality characteristic that tends to lead to certain behaviors is called a

trait. The term trait also means a genetically inherited feature of an organism.

Nucleus	In neuroanatomy, a cluster of cell bodies of neurons within the central nervous system is a nucleus.
Homozygous	When an organism is referred to as being homozygous for a specific gene, it means that it carries two identical copies of that gene for a given trait on the two corresponding chromosomes (e.g., the genotype is AA or aa). Such a cell or an organism is called a homozygote.
Heterozygous	Heterozygous refers to the condition in which a pair of genes occupying the same locus on a pair of chromosomes are different from one another.
Allele	An allele is any one of a number of alternative forms of the same gene (sometimes the term refers to a non-gene sequence) occupying a given locus (position) on a chromosome.
Dominant allele	The dominant allele, of two alleles for the same trait, is the one that is expressed in a heterozygote. Many traits are determined by pairs of complementary genes, each inherited from a single parent. Often when these are paired and compared, one gene will be found to effectively shut out the instructions from the other gene.
Recessive allele	Recessive allele refers to an unexpressed allele in a heterozygote, but is phenotypically expressed when homozygous (an organism that has two copies of the same allele).. Thus, both parents have to be carriers of a recessive trait in order for a child to express that trait.
Shyness	A tendency to avoid others plus uneasiness and strain when socializing is called shyness.
Recessive gene	Recessive gene refers to an allele that causes a phenotype (visible or detectable characteristic) that is only seen in a homozygous genotype (an organism that has two copies of the same allele). Thus, both parents have to be carriers of a recessive trait in order for a child to express that trait.
Dominant gene	In genetics, the term dominant gene refers to the allele that causes a phenotype that is seen in a heterozygous genotype.
Color blindness	Color blindness in humans is the inability to perceive differences between some or all colors that other people can distinguish. It is most often of genetic nature, but may also occur because of eye, nerve, or brain damage, or due to exposure to certain chemicals.
Retina	The retina is a thin layer of cells at the back of the eyeball. It is the part of the eye which converts light into nervous signals. The retina contains photoreceptor cells which receive the light; the resulting neural signals then undergo complex processing by other neurons of the retina, and are transformed into action potentials in retinal ganglion cells whose axons form the optic nerve.
Individual differences	Individual differences psychology studies the ways in which individual people differ in their behavior. This is distinguished from other aspects of psychology in that although psychology is ostensibly a study of individuals, modern psychologists invariably study groups.
Sensorimotor	The first of Piaget's stages is the Sensorimotor stage. This stage typically ranges from birth to 2 years. In this stage, children experience the world through their senses. During this stage, object permanence and stranger anxiety develop.
Canalization	Canalization refers to the process by which characteristics take a narrow path over a developmental course.
Genetics	Genetics is the science of genes, heredity, and the variation of organisms.
Attention	Attention is the cognitive process of selectively concentrating on one thing while ignoring other things. Psychologists have labeled three types of attention: sustained attention, selective attention, and divided attention.

Deprivation	Deprivation, is the loss or withholding of normal stimulation, nutrition, comfort, love, and so forth; a condition of lacking. The level of stimulation is less than what is required.
Variability	Statistically, variability refers to how much the scores in a distribution spread out, away from the mean.
Personality	Personality refers to the pattern of enduring characteristics that differentiates a person, the patterns of behaviors that make each individual unique.
Personality trait	According to the Diagnostic and Statistical Manual of the American Psychiatric Association, a personality trait is a "prominent aspect of personality that is exhibited in a wide range of important social and personal contexts. ...".
Heritability	Heritability It is that proportion of the observed variation in a particular phenotype within a particular population, that can be attributed to the contribution of genotype. In other words: it measures the extent to which differences between individuals in a population are due their being different genetically.
Population	Population refers to all members of a well-defined group of organisms, events, or things.
Variance	The degree to which scores differ among individuals in a distribution of scores is the variance.
Statistic	A statistic is an observable random variable of a sample.
Kinship studies	Kinship studies compare the presence of traits and behavior patterns in people who are biologically related or unrelated in order to help determine the role of genetic factors in their occurrence.
Correlation	A statistical technique for determining the degree of association between two or more variables is referred to as correlation.
Mental illness	Mental illness is the term formerly used to mean psychological disorder but less preferred because it implies that the causes of the disorder can be found in a medical disease process.
Quantitative	A quantitative property is one that exists in a range of magnitudes, and can therefore be measured. Measurements of any particular quantitative property are expressed as as a specific quantity, referred to as a unit, multiplied by a number.
Hypertension	Hypertension is a medical condition where the blood pressure in the arteries is chronically elevated. Persistent hypertension is one of the risk factors for strokes, heart attacks, heart failure and arterial aneurysm, and is a leading cause of chronic renal failure.
Depression	In everyday language depression refers to any downturn in mood, which may be relatively transitory and perhaps due to something trivial. This is differentiated from Clinical depression which is marked by symptoms that last two weeks or more and are so severe that they interfere with daily living.
Diabetes	Diabetes is a medical disorder characterized by varying or persistent elevated blood sugar levels, especially after eating. All types of diabetes share similar symptoms and complications at advanced stages: dehydration and ketoacidosis, cardiovascular disease, chronic renal failure, retinal damage which can lead to blindness, nerve damage which can lead to erectile dysfunction, gangrene with risk of amputation of toes, feet, and even legs.
Asthma	Asthma is a complex disease characterized by bronchial hyperresponsiveness (BHR), inflammation, mucus production and intermittent airway obstruction.
Family studies	Scientific studies in which researchers assess hereditary influence by examining blood relatives to see how much they resemble each other on a specific trait are called family studies.

Twin study	A twin study is a kind of genetic study done to determine heritability. The premise is that since identical twins (especially identical twins raised apart) have identical genotypes, differences between them are solely due to environmental factors. By examining the degree to which twins are differentiated, a study may determine the extent to which a particular trait is influenced by genes or the environment.
Metabolism	Metabolism is the biochemical modification of chemical compounds in living organisms and cells.
Alcoholism	A disorder that involves long-term, repeated, uncontrolled, compulsive, and excessive use of alcoholic beverages and that impairs the drinker's health and work and social relationships is called alcoholism.
Eugenics	The field concerned with improving the hereditary qualities of the human race through social control of mating and reproduction is called eugenics.
Human genome	The complete sequence or mapping of genes in the human body and their locations is the human genome. It is made up of 23 chromosome pairs with a total of about 3 billion DNA base pairs.
Human genome project	The Human Genome Project endeavored to map the human genome down to the nucleotide (or base pair) level and to identify all the genes present in it.
Immune response	The body's defensive reaction to invasion by bacteria, viral agents, or other foreign substances is called the immune response.
Adoption studies	Research studies that assess hereditary influence by examining the resemblance between adopted children and both their biological and their adoptive parents are referred to as adoption studies. The studies have been inconclusive about the relative importance of heredity in intelligence.
Heredity	Heredity is the transfer of characteristics from parent to offspring through their genes.
Mutation	Mutation is a permanent, sometimes transmissible (if the change is to a germ cell) change to the genetic material (usually DNA or RNA) of a cell. They can be caused by copying errors in the genetic material during cell division and by exposure to radiation, chemicals, or viruses, or can occur deliberately under cellular control during the processes such as meiosis or hypermutation.
Affect	A subjective feeling or emotional tone often accompanied by bodily expressions noticeable to others is called affect.
Phenylketonuria	Phenylketonuria is a genetic disorder in which an individual cannot properly metabolize amino acids. The disorder is now easily detected but, if left untreated, results in mental retardation and hyperactivity.
Down syndrome	Down syndrome encompasses a number of genetic disorders, of which trisomy 21 (a nondisjunction, the so-called extrachromosone) is the most representative, causing highly variable degrees of learning difficulties as well as physical disabilities. Incidence of Down syndrome is estimated at 1 per 660 births, making it the most common chromosomal abnormality.
Trisomy	A condition wherein there are three rather than the usual pair of homologous chromosomes within the cell nucleus is referred to as trisomy.
Severe mental retardation	A limitation in mental development as measured on the Wechsler Adult Intelligence Scale with scores between 20 -34 is called severe mental retardation.
Mental retardation	Mental retardation refers to having significantly below-average intellectual functioning and limitations in at least two areas of adaptive functioning. Many categorize retardation as mild, moderate, severe, or profound.
Metabolic	A metabolic disorder is a medical disorder which affects the production of energy within

disorder	individual human (or animal) cells. Most metabolic disorders are genetic, though a few are "acquired" as a result of diet, toxins, infections, etc.
Phenylalanine	Phenylalanine is an essential amino acid. The genetic disorder phenylketonuria is an inability to metabolize phenylalanine.
Amino acid	Amino acid is the basic structural building unit of proteins. They form short polymer chains called peptides or polypeptides which in turn form structures called proteins.
Tyrosine	Tyrosine is one of the 20 amino acids that are used by cells to synthesize proteins. It plays a key role in signal transduction, since it can be tagged (phosphorylated) with a phosphate group by protein kinases to alter the functionality and activity of certain enzymes.
Brain	The brain controls and coordinates most movement, behavior and homeostatic body functions such as heartbeat, blood pressure, fluid balance and body temperature. Functions of the brain are responsible for cognition, emotion, memory, motor learning and other sorts of learning. The brain is primarily made up of two types of cells: glia and neurons.
Prefrontal cortex	The prefrontal cortex is the anterior part of the frontal lobes of the brain, lying in front of the motor and associative areas. It has been implicated in planning complex cognitive behaviors, personality expression and moderating correct social behavior. The prefrontal cortex continues to develop until around age 6.
Hypothesis	A specific statement about behavior or mental processes that is testable through research is a hypothesis.
Genetic testing	Genetic testing allows the genetic diagnosis of vulnerabilities to inherited diseases, and can also be used to determine a person's ancestry. Every person carries two copies of every gene, one inherited from their mother, one inherited from their father.
Counselor	A counselor is a mental health professional who specializes in helping people with problems not involving serious mental disorders.
Genetic counseling	Genetic counseling generally refers to prenatal counseling done when a genetic condition is suspected in a pregnancy. Genetic counseling is the process by which patients or relatives at risk of an inherited disorder are advised of the consequences and nature of the disorder, the probability of developing or transmitting it, and the options open to them in management and family planning in order to prevent, avoid or ameliorate it.
Postnatal	Postnatal is the period beginning immediately after the birth of a child and extending for about six weeks. The period is also known as postpartum and, less commonly, puerperium.
Prenatal	Prenatal period refers to the time from conception to birth.
Anesthesia	Anesthesia is the process of blocking the perception of pain and other sensations. This allows patients to undergo surgery and other procedures without the distress and pain they would otherwise experience.
Testosterone	Testosterone is a steroid hormone from the androgen group. It is the principal male sex hormone and the "original" anabolic steroid.
Adolescence	The period of life bounded by puberty and the assumption of adult responsibilities is adolescence.
Hormone	A hormone is a chemical messenger from one cell (or group of cells) to another. The best known are those produced by endocrine glands, but they are produced by nearly every organ system. The function of hormones is to serve as a signal to the target cells; the action of the hormone is determined by the pattern of secretion and the signal transduction of the receiving tissue.
Meme	By analogy to genetics, a meme is passed from generation to generation, with occasional

29

	"mutations," but is passed via family and cultural traditions or training rather than sexual reproduction. Dawkins defined meme as a unit of cultural transmission, a unit of imitation.
Society	The social sciences use the term society to mean a group of people that form a semi-closed (or semi-open) social system, in which most interactions are with other individuals belonging to the group.
Frontal lobe	The frontal lobe comprises four major folds of cortical tissue: the precentral gyrus, superior gyrus and the middle gyrus of the frontal gyri, the inferior frontal gyrus. It has been found to play a part in impulse control, judgement, language, memory, motor function, problem solving, sexual behavior, socialization and spontaneity.
Lobes	The four major sections of the cerebral cortex: frontal, parietal, temporal, and occipital are called lobes.
Shaping	The concept of reinforcing successive, increasingly accurate approximations to a target behavior is called shaping. The target behavior is broken down into a hierarchy of elemental steps, each step more sophisticated then the last. By successively reinforcing each of the the elemental steps, a form of differential reinforcement, until that step is learned while extinguishing the step below, the target behavior is gradually achieved.
Inference	Inference is the act or process of drawing a conclusion based solely on what one already knows.
Adaptation	Adaptation is a lowering of sensitivity to a stimulus following prolonged exposure to that stimulus. Behavioral adaptations are special ways a particular organism behaves to survive in its natural habitat.
Nurture	Nurture refers to the environmental influences on behavior due to nutrition, culture, socioeconomic status, and learning.

Society	The social sciences use the term society to mean a group of people that form a semi-closed (or semi-open) social system, in which most interactions are with other individuals belonging to the group.
Zygote	A zygote is a cell that is the result of fertilization. That is, two haploid cells—usually (but not always) a sperm cell from a male and an ovum from a female—merge into a single diploid cell called the zygote.
Prenatal	Prenatal period refers to the time from conception to birth.
Habit	A habit is a response that has become completely separated from its eliciting stimulus. Early learning theorists used the term to describe S-R associations, however not all S-R associations become a habit, rather many are extinguished after reinforcement is withdrawn.
Ovum	Ovum is a female sex cell or gamete.
Chromosome	The DNA which carries genetic information in biological cells is normally packaged in the form of one or more large macromolecules called a chromosome. Humans normally have 46.
Nucleus	In neuroanatomy, a cluster of cell bodies of neurons within the central nervous system is a nucleus.
Gene	A gene is an ultramicroscopic area of the chromosome. It is the smallest physical unit of the DNA molecule that carries a piece of hereditary information.
Zona pellucida	The zona pellucida is a glycoprotein matrix surrounding the plasma membrane of an oocyte. This structure binds spermatozoa, and is required to initiate the acrosome reaction. The enzyme layer that surrounds the egg only reacts with sperm that have matching enzymes, keeping sperm of other species from fertilizing the egg.
Embryonic period	Embryonic period refers to the period of prenatal development that occurs 2 to 8 weeks after conception. During the embryonic period, the rate of cell differentiation intensifies, support systems for the cells form, and organs appear.
Germinal period	The germinal period refers to the period of prenatal development that takes place in the first 2 weeks after conception. It includes the creation of the zygote, continued cell division, and the attachment of the zygote to the uterine wall.
Fetal period	The prenatal period of development that begins 2 months after conception and lasts for 7 months, on the average is called the fetal period.
Uterus	The uterus or womb is the major female reproductive organ. The main function of the uterus is to accept a fertilized ovum which becomes implanted into the endometrium, and derives nourishment from blood vessels which develop exclusively for this purpose.
Fallopian tube	A tube through which the eggs travel from the ovaries to the uterus is a fallopian tube.
Blastocyst	The Blastocyst si an inner layer of cells that develops during the germinal period. These cells later develop into the embryo.
Stages	Stages represent relatively discrete periods of time in which functioning is qualitatively different from functioning at other periods.
Variability	Statistically, variability refers to how much the scores in a distribution spread out, away from the mean.
Stem cells	Stem cells are primal undifferentiated cells which retain the ability to differentiate into other cell types. This ability allows them to act as a repair system for the body, replenishing other cells as long as the organism is alive.
Embryo	A developed zygote that has a rudimentary heart, brain, and other organs is referred to as an embryo.

Go to **Cram101.com** for the Practice Tests for this Chapter.

Trophoblast	The trophoblast is the outer layer of cells that develops in the germinal period. These cells provide nutrition and support for the embryo.
Attention	Attention is the cognitive process of selectively concentrating on one thing while ignoring other things. Psychologists have labeled three types of attention: sustained attention, selective attention, and divided attention.
Mesoderm	The mesoderm is one of the three germ layers in the early developing embryo. The mesoderm gives rise to tissues including connective tissue, muscles and the circulatory system.
Endoderm	The endoderm is one of the three germ layers of the developing embryo, the other two being the ectoderm and the mesoderm. The endoderm gives rise to various tissues including the gastrointestinal tract, respiratory tract, and endocrine glands.
Ectoderm	Ectoderm refers to the outermost cell layer of the newly formed embryo, from which the skin and nervous systems develop.
Epigenesis	The emergence of new structures and functions, during the course of development is referred to as epigenesis.
Amniotic fluid	Amniotic fluid refers to fluid within the amniotic sac that suspends and protects the fetus.
Amnion	The amniotic sac is a tough but thin transparent pair of membranes, which hold a developing embryo (and later fetus) until shortly before birth. The inner membrane, the amnion, contains the amniotic fluid and the fetus.
Placenta	A membrane that permits the exchange of nutrients and waste products between the mother and her developing child but does not allow the maternal and fetal bloodstreams to mix is the placenta.
Chorion	The amniotic sac is a tough but thin transparent pair of membranes, which hold a developing embryo (and later fetus) until shortly before birth. The inner membrane, the amnion, contains the amniotic fluid and the fetus. The outer membrane, the chorion, contains the amnion and is part of the placenta.
Umbilical cord	The umbilical cord is a tube that connects a developing embryo or fetus to its placenta. It contains major arteries and veins for the exchange of nutrient- and oxygen-rich blood between the embryo and placenta.
Cephalocaudal	The sequence in which the greatest growth occurs at the top, the head, with physical growth in size, weight, and feature differentiation gradually working from top to bottom is referred to as a cephalocaudal pattern.
Proximodistal	Development originating from the center of the body towards the extremities is referred to as proximodistal development. The human embroyo normally develops in this fashion and averages 5-10 pounds in brith-weight and between 18 to 22 inches in length.
Spinal cord	The spinal cord is a part of the vertebrate nervous system that is enclosed in and protected by the vertebral column (it passes through the spinal canal). It consists of nerve cells. The spinal cord carries sensory signals and motor innervation to most of the skeletal muscles in the body.
Brain	The brain controls and coordinates most movement, behavior and homeostatic body functions such as heartbeat, blood pressure, fluid balance and body temperature. Functions of the brain are responsible for cognition, emotion, memory, motor learning and other sorts of learning. The brain is primarily made up of two types of cells: glia and neurons.
Nerve	A nerve is an enclosed, cable-like bundle of nerve fibers or axons, which includes the glia that ensheath the axons in myelin. Neurons are sometimes called nerve cells, though this term is technically imprecise since many neurons do not form nerves.

Lungs	The lungs are the essential organs of respiration. Its principal function is to transport oxygen from the atmosphere into the bloodstream, and excrete carbon dioxide from the bloodstream into the atmosphere.
Inner ear	The inner ear consists of the oval window, cochlea, and basilar membrane.
Fetus	A fetus develops from the end of the 8th week of pregnancy (when the major structures have formed), until birth.
Nervous system	The body's electrochemical communication circuitry, made up of billions of neurons is a nervous system.
Central nervous system	The vertebrate central nervous system consists of the brain and spinal cord.
X chromosome	The sex chromosomes are one of the 23 pairs of human chromosomes. Each person normally has one pair of sex chromosomes in each cell. Females have two X chromosomes, while males have one X and one Y chromosome. The X chromosome carries hundreds of genes but few, if any, of these have anything to do directly with sex determination.
Y chromosome	The Y chromosome is one of the two sex chromosomes in humans and most other mammals. The sex chromosomes are one of the 23 pairs of human chromosomes. The Y chromosome contains the fewest genes of any of the chromosomes. It contains the genes that cause testis development, thus determining maleness. It is usually contributed by the father.
Gonads	The gonads are the organs that make gametes. Gametes are haploid germ cells. For example, sperm and egg cells are gametes. In the male the gonads are the testicles, and in the female the gonads are the ovaries.
Gland	A gland is an organ in an animal's body that synthesizes a substance for release such as hormones, often into the bloodstream or into cavities inside the body or its outer surface.
Testes	Testes are the male reproductive glands or gonads; this is where sperm develop and are stored.
Ovary	The female reproductive organ is the ovary. It performs two major functions: producing eggs and secreting hormones.
Genitals	Genitals refers to the internal and external reproductive organs.
Androgen	Androgen is the generic term for any natural or synthetic compound, usually a steroid hormone, that stimulates or controls the development and maintenance of masculine characteristics in vertebrates by binding to androgen receptors.
Hormone	A hormone is a chemical messenger from one cell (or group of cells) to another. The best known are those produced by endocrine glands, but they are produced by nearly every organ system. The function of hormones is to serve as a signal to the target cells; the action of the hormone is determined by the pattern of secretion and the signal transduction of the receiving tissue.
Testosterone	Testosterone is a steroid hormone from the androgen group. It is the principal male sex hormone and the "original" anabolic steroid.
Scrotum	The scrotum is an external sack of skin that holds the testes.
Penis	The penis is the external male copulatory organ and the external male organ of urination. In humans, the penis is homologous to the female clitoris, as it develops from the same embryonic structure. It is capable of erection for use in copulation.
Pituitary gland	The pituitary gland is an endocrine gland about the size of a pea that sits in the small, bony cavity at the base of the brain. The pituitary gland secretes hormones regulating a wide

variety of bodily activities, including trophic hormones that stimulate other endocrine glands.

Hermaphrodite	Hermaphrodite refers to a person with parts of both male and female genitalia.
Affect	A subjective feeling or emotional tone often accompanied by bodily expressions noticeable to others is called affect.
Amniotic sac	The amniotic sac is a tough but thin transparent pair of membranes, which hold a developing embryo (and later fetus) until shortly before birth. The inner membrane, the amnion, contains the amniotic fluid and the fetus.
Middle ear	The middle ear consists of the eardrum, hammer, anvil, and stirrup.
Vestibular system	The vestibular system, or balance system, is the sensory system that provides the dominant input about our movement and orientation in space. Together with the cochlea, the auditory organ, it is situated in the vestibulum in the inner ear.
Maturation	The orderly unfolding of traits, as regulated by the genetic code is called maturation.
Neuron	The neuron is the primary cell of the nervous system. They are found in the brain, the spinal cord, in the nerves and ganglia of the peripheral nervous system. It is a specialized cell that conducts impulses through the nervous system and contains three major parts: cell body, dendrites, and an axon. It can have many dendrites but only one axon.
Learning	Learning is a relatively permanent change in behavior that results from experience. Thus, to attribute a behavioral change to learning, the change must be relatively permanent and must result from experience.
Cerebral hemisphere	Either of the two halves that make up the cerebrum is referred to as a cerebral hemisphere. The hemispheres operate together, linked by the corpus callosum, a very large bundle of nerve fibers, and also by other smaller commissures.
Spence	Spence attributed improvement in performance to motivational factors rather than habit factors. His Discrimination Learning Theory argued that reinforcement combined with frustration or inhibitors facilitates finding a correct stimulus among a cluster which includes incorrect ones.
Cowan	Cowan regards working memory not as a separate system, but as a part of long-term memory. Representations in working memory are a subset of the representations in long-term memory.
Baseline	Measure of a particular behavior or process taken before the introduction of the independent variable or treatment is called the baseline.
Attitude	An enduring mental representation of a person, place, or thing that evokes an emotional response and related behavior is called attitude.
Control group	A group that does not receive the treatment effect in an experiment is referred to as the control group or sometimes as the comparison group.
Socioeconomic	Socioeconomic pertains to the study of the social and economic impacts of any product or service offering, market intervention or other activity on an economy as a whole and on the companies, organization and individuals who are its main economic actors.
Socioeconomic Status	A family's socioeconomic status is based on family income, parental education level, parental occupation, and social status in the community. Those with high status often have more success in preparing their children for school because they have access to a wide range of resources.
Adrenaline	Adrenaline refers to a hormone produced by the adrenal medulla that stimulates sympathetic ANS activity and generally arouses people and heightens their emotional responsiveness.

Cortisol	Cortisol is a corticosteroid hormone that is involved in the response to stress; it increases blood pressure and blood sugar levels and suppresses the immune system. Synthetic cortisol, also known as hydrocortisone, is used as a drug mainly to fight allergies and inflammation.
Low birth weight	Low birth weight is a fetus that weighs less than 2500 g (5 lb 8 oz) regardless of gestational age.
Malnutrition	Malnutrition is a general term for the medical condition in a person or animal caused by an unbalanced diet—either too little or too much food, or a diet missing one or more important nutrients.
Population	Population refers to all members of a well-defined group of organisms, events, or things.
Deprivation	Deprivation, is the loss or withholding of normal stimulation, nutrition, comfort, love, and so forth; a condition of lacking. The level of stimulation is less than what is required.
Metabolism	Metabolism is the biochemical modification of chemical compounds in living organisms and cells.
Physiology	The study of the functions and activities of living cells, tissues, and organs and of the physical and chemical phenomena involved is referred to as physiology.
Adaptation	Adaptation is a lowering of sensitivity to a stimulus following prolonged exposure to that stimulus. Behavioral adaptations are special ways a particular organism behaves to survive in its natural habitat.
Stroke	A stroke occurs when the blood supply to a part of the brain is suddenly interrupted by occlusion, by hemorrhage, or other causes
Sensitive period	A sensitive period is a developmental window in which a predisposed behavior is most likely to develop given appropriate stimulation. In linguistic theory, the period from about 18 months to puberty is when the brain is thought to be primed for learning language because of plasticity of the brain.
Infancy	The developmental period that extends from birth to 18 or 24 months is called infancy.
Postnatal	Postnatal is the period beginning immediately after the birth of a child and extending for about six weeks. The period is also known as postpartum and, less commonly, puerperium.
Teratogen	Teratogen refers to from the Greek word tera, meaning 'monster.' It is any agent that causes a birth defect.
Teratogenic	Capacity for causing birth defects is referred to as teratogenic.
Critical period	A period of time when an innate response can be elicited by a particular stimulus is referred to as the critical period.
Cerebral palsy	Cerebral palsy is a group of permanent disorders associated with developmental brain injuries that occur during fetal development, birth, or shortly after birth. It is characterized by a disruption of motor skills, with symptoms such as spasticity, paralysis, or seizures.
Thalidomide	Thalidomide is a drug which was sold during the 1950s and 1960s as a sleeping aid and to pregnant women as an antiemetic to combat morning sickness and other symptoms. It was later (1960–61) found to be teratogenic in fetal development, most visibly as a cause of amelia or phocomelia.
Mercury	Elemental, liquid mercury is slightly toxic, while its vapor, compounds and salts are highly toxic and have been implicated as causing brain and liver damage when ingested, inhaled or contacted. Because mercury is easily transferred across the placenta, the embryo is highly susceptible to birth defects.
Diabetes	Diabetes is a medical disorder characterized by varying or persistent elevated blood sugar

Go to **Cram101.com** for the Practice Tests for this Chapter.

Go to **Cram101.com** for the Practice Tests for this Chapter.
And, **NEVER** highlight a book again!

	levels, especially after eating. All types of diabetes share similar symptoms and complications at advanced stages: dehydration and ketoacidosis, cardiovascular disease, chronic renal failure, retinal damage which can lead to blindness, nerve damage which can lead to erectile dysfunction, gangrene with risk of amputation of toes, feet, and even legs.
Liver	The liver plays a major role in metabolism and has a number of functions in the body including detoxification, glycogen storage and plasma protein synthesis. It also produces bile, which is important for digestion. The liver converts most carbohydrates, proteing, and fats into glucose.
Rubella	An infectious disease that, if contracted by the mother during the first three months of pregnancy, has a high risk of causing mental retardation and physical deformity in the child is called rubella.
Sedative	A sedative is a drug that depresses the central nervous system (CNS), which causes calmness, relaxation, reduction of anxiety, sleepiness, slowed breathing, slurred speech, staggering gait, poor judgment, and slow, uncertain reflexes.
Schizophrenia	Schizophrenia is characterized by persistent defects in the perception or expression of reality. A person suffering from untreated schizophrenia typically demonstrates grossly disorganized thinking, and may also experience delusions or auditory hallucinations
Tranquilizer	A sedative, or tranquilizer, is a drug that depresses the central nervous system (CNS), which causes calmness, relaxation, reduction of anxiety, sleepiness, slowed breathing, slurred speech, staggering gait, poor judgment, and slow, uncertain reflexes.
Thorazine	Thorazine is the trade name for chlorpromazine, one of the antipsychotic drugs and a member of the phenothiazine group. It is classified as a low-potency antipsychotic and is used in the treatment of both acute and chronic psychoses, including schizophrenia and the manic phase of manic depression.
Spontaneous abortion	Spontaneous abortion is the natural or accidental termination of a pregnancy at a stage where the embryo or the fetus is incapable of surviving, generally defined at a gestation less than 20 weeks.
Nicotine	Nicotine is an organic compound, an alkaloid found naturally throughout the tobacco plant, with a high concentration in the leaves. It is a potent nerve poison and is included in many insecticides. In lower concentrations, the substance is a stimulant and is one of the main factors leading to the pleasure and habit-forming qualities of tobacco smoking.
Alcoholism	A disorder that involves long-term, repeated, uncontrolled, compulsive, and excessive use of alcoholic beverages and that impairs the drinker's health and work and social relationships is called alcoholism.
Congenital	A condition existing at birth is referred to as congenital.
Syndrome	The term syndrome is the association of several clinically recognizable features, signs, symptoms, phenomena or characteristics which often occur together, so that the presence of one feature indicates the presence of the others.
Fetal alcohol syndrome	A cluster of abnormalities that appears in the offspring of mothers who drink alcohol heavily during pregnancy is called fetal alcohol syndrome.
Binge drinking	Binge drinking refers to consuming 5 or more drinks in a short time or drinking alchohol for the sole purpose of intoxication.
Adolescence	The period of life bounded by puberty and the assumption of adult responsibilities is adolescence.
Binge	Binge refers to relatively brief episode of uncontrolled, excessive consumption.

Marijuana	Marijuana is the dried vegetable matter of the Cannabis sativa plant. It contains large concentrations of compounds that have medicinal and psychoactive effects when consumed, usually by smoking or eating.
Survey	A method of scientific investigation in which a large sample of people answer questions about their attitudes or behavior is referred to as a survey.
Addiction	Addiction is an uncontrollable compulsion to repeat a behavior regardless of its consequences. Many drugs or behaviors can precipitate a pattern of conditions recognized as addiction, which include a craving for more of the drug or behavior, increased physiological tolerance to exposure, and withdrawal symptoms in the absence of the stimulus.
Stimulant	A stimulant is a drug which increases the activity of the sympathetic nervous system and produces a sense of euphoria or awakeness.
Cocaine	Cocaine is a crystalline tropane alkaloid that is obtained from the leaves of the coca plant. It is a stimulant of the central nervous system and an appetite suppressant, creating what has been described as a euphoric sense of happiness and increased energy.
Seizure	A seizure is a temporary alteration in brain function expressed as a changed mental state, tonic or clonic movements and various other symptoms. They are due to temporary abnormal electrical activity of a group of brain cells.
Methadone	Methadone is a synthetic heroin substitute used for treating heroin addicts that acts as a substitute for heroin by eliminating its effects and the craving for it. Just like heroin, tolerance and dependence frequently develop.
Heroin	Heroin is widely and illegally used as a powerful and addictive drug producing intense euphoria, which often disappears with increasing tolerance. Heroin is a semi-synthetic opioid. It is the 3,6-diacetyl derivative of morphine and is synthesised from it by acetylation.
Placental barrier	The placental barrier between the fetus and the wall of the mother's uterus allows for the transfer of materials from mother, and eliminates waste products of fetus.
Sexually Transmitted Disease	Sexually transmitted disease is commonly transmitted between partners through some form of sexual activity, most commonly vaginal intercourse, oral sex, or anal sex.
Genital herpes	Genital herpes refers to a sexually transmitted disease caused by a large family of viruses of different strains. These strains also produce other, nonsexually transmitted diseases such as chicken pox and mononucleosis.
Lesion	A lesion is a non-specific term referring to abnormal tissue in the body. It can be caused by any disease process including trauma (physical, chemical, electrical), infection, neoplasm, metabolic and autoimmune.
Gonorrhea	Gonorrhea is among the most common curable sexually transmitted diseases in the world. In men, epididymitis, prostatitis and urethral stricture can result from untreated gonorrhoea.In women, Bartholinitis and abscess formation, pelvic inflammatory disease and Fitz-Hugh-Curtis syndrome can occur.
Syphilis	Syphilis is a sexually transmitted disease that is caused by a spirochaete bacterium, Treponema pallidum. If not treated, syphilis can cause serious effects such as damage to the nervous system, heart, or brain. Untreated syphilis can be ultimately fatal.
Chronic	Chronic refers to a relatively long duration, usually more than a few months.
Protein	A protein is a complex, high-molecular-weight organic compound that consists of amino acids joined by peptide bonds. It is essential to the structure and function of all living cells

Go to **Cram101.com** for the Practice Tests for this Chapter.

and viruses. Many are enzymes or subunits of enzymes.

Toxemia	Toxemia is another term for blood poisoning, or the presence in the bloodstream of quantities of bacteria or bacterial toxins sufficient to cause serious illness.
Acquired immunodeficiency syndrome	Acquired Immunodeficiency Syndrome is defined as a collection of symptoms and infections resulting from the depletion of the immune system caused by infection with the human immunodeficiency virus, commonly called HIV.
UNICEF	UNICEF, the United Nations International Children's Emergency Fund, was established by the United Nations General Assembly on December 11, 1946. UNICEF provides long-term humanitarian and developmental assistance to children and mothers in developing countries.
Dominant gene	In genetics, the term dominant gene refers to the allele that causes a phenotype that is seen in a heterozygous genotype.
Recessive gene	Recessive gene refers to an allele that causes a phenotype (visible or detectable characteristic) that is only seen in a homozygous genotype (an organism that has two copies of the same allele). Thus, both parents have to be carriers of a recessive trait in order for a child to express that trait.
Immune system	The most important function of the human immune system occurs at the cellular level of the blood and tissues. The lymphatic and blood circulation systems are highways for specialized white blood cells. These cells include B cells, T cells, natural killer cells, and macrophages. All function with the primary objective of recognizing, attacking and destroying bacteria, viruses, cancer cells, and all substances seen as foreign.
Antibody	An antibody is a protein used by the immune system to identify and neutralize foreign objects like bacteria and viruses. Each antibody recognizes a specific antigen unique to its target.
Trauma	Trauma refers to a severe physical injury or wound to the body caused by an external force, or a psychological shock having a lasting effect on mental life.
Psychological trauma	Psychological trauma involves a singular experience or enduring event or events that completely overwhelm the individual's ability to cope or integrate the emotion involved with that experience. It usually involves a complete feeling of helplessness in the face of a real or subjective threat to life, bodily integrity, or sanity.
Regression	Return to a form of behavior characteristic of an earlier stage of development is called regression.
Cervix	The cervix is the lower end of the uterus that joins with the top portion of the vaginia.
Construct	A generalized concept, such as anxiety or gravity, is a construct.
Breech position	The baby's position in the uterus that causes the buttocks to be the first part to emerge from the vagina is a breech position.
Midwife	A Midwife is a blanket term used to describe a number of different types of health practitioners, other than physicians, who provide prenatal care to expecting mothers, attend the birth of the infant and provide postnatal care to the mother and infant.
Sympathetic	The sympathetic nervous system activates what is often termed the "fight or flight response". It is an automatic regulation system, that is, one that operates without the intervention of conscious thought.
Cesarean section	A cesarean section is a form of childbirth in which a surgical incision is made through a mother's abdomen and uterus to deliver one or more babies. It is usually performed when a vaginal delivery would lead to medical complications.
Anesthesia	Anesthesia is the process of blocking the perception of pain and other sensations. This

Go to **Cram101.com** for the Practice Tests for this Chapter.

allows patients to undergo surgery and other procedures without the distress and pain they would otherwise experience.

Stress hormones	Group of hormones including cortico steroids, that are involved in the body's physiological stress response are referred to as stress hormones.
Metabolic rate	Metabolic rate refers to the rate at which the body burns calories to produce energy.
Apgar scale	The Apgar scale is a simple and repeatable method to quickly and assess the health of newborn children immediately after childbirth. The test is generally done at one and five minutes after birth, and may be repeated later if the score is, and remains, low. Scores below 3 are generally regarded as critically low, with 4 to 7 fairly low and over 7 generally normal.
Reflex	A simple, involuntary response to a stimulus is referred to as reflex. Reflex actions originate at the spinal cord rather than the brain.
Brazelton	Brazelton Neonatal Behavioral Assessment Scale is a test given several days after birth to assess newborns' neurological development, reflexes, and reactions to people.
Preterm	Born at or prior to completion of 37 weeks of gestation is referred to as preterm.
Personality	Personality refers to the pattern of enduring characteristics that differentiates a person, the patterns of behaviors that make each individual unique.
Acute	Acute means sudden, sharp, and abrupt. Usually short in duration.
Preterm infant	An infant born before completing the thirty-seventh week of gestation is a preterm infant.
Emotion	An emotion is a mental states that arise spontaneously, rather than through conscious effort. They are often accompanied by physiological changes.
Narcotic	The term narcotic originally referred to a variety of substances that induced sleep (such state is narcosis). In legal context, narcotic refers to opium, opium derivatives, and their semisynthetic or totally synthetic substitutes.
Graham	Graham has conducted a number of studies that reveal stronger socioeconomic-status influences rather than ethnic influences in achievement.
Social ecology	The entire network of interactions and interdependencies among people, institutions, and cultural constructs to which the developing person must adapt psychologically is called the social ecology.
Ecology	Ecology refers to the branch of biology that deals with the relationships between living organisms and their environment.
Species	Species refers to a reproductively isolated breeding population.
Experimental group	Experimental group refers to any group receiving a treatment effect in an experiment.
Analogy	An analogy is a comparison between two different things, in order to highlight some form of similarity. Analogy is the cognitive process of transferring information from a particular subject to another particular subject.
Attachment	Attachment is the tendency to seek closeness to another person and feel secure when that person is present.
Ethology	Where comparative psychology sees the study of animal behavior in the context of what is known about human psychology, ethology sees the study of animal behavior in the context of what is known about animal anatomy and physiology.
Lorenz	Lorenz demonstrated how incubator-hatched geese would imprint on the first suitable moving stimulus they saw within what he called a "critical period" of about 36 hours shortly after

hatching. Most famously, the goslings would imprint on Lorenz himself .

Physiological changes	Alterations in heart rate, blood pressure, perspiration, and other involuntary responses are physiological changes.
Distinctive features	The characteristics of an object that differentiate it from other objects are distinctive features.
Ultrasound	Ultrasound is sound with a frequency greater than the upper limit of human hearing, approximately 20 kilohertz. Medical use can visualise muscle and soft tissue, making them useful for scanning the organs, and obstetric ultrasonography is commonly used during pregnancy.
Senses	The senses are systems that consist of a sensory cell type that respond to a specific kind of physical energy, and that correspond to a defined region within the brain where the signals are received and interpreted.
Hypothesis	A specific statement about behavior or mental processes that is testable through research is a hypothesis.
Motor neuron	A motor neuron is an efferent neuron that originates in the spinal cord and synapses with muscle fibers to facilitate muscle contraction and with muscle spindles to modify proprioceptive sensitivity.
Frontal lobe	The frontal lobe comprises four major folds of cortical tissue: the precentral gyrus, superior gyrus and the middle gyrus of the frontal gyri, the inferior frontal gyrus. It has been found to play a part in impulse control, judgement, language, memory, motor function, problem solving, sexual behavior, socialization and spontaneity.
Hippocampus	The hippocampus is a part of the brain located inside the temporal lobe. It forms a part of the limbic system and plays a part in memory and navigation.
Myelination	The process in which the nerve cells are covered and insulated with a layer of fat cells, which increases the speed at which information travels through the nervous system is referred to as myelination.
Cerebellum	The cerebellum is located in the inferior posterior portion of the head (the hindbrain), directly dorsal to the brainstem and pons, inferior to the occipital lobe. The cerebellum is a region of the brain that plays an important role in the integration of sensory perception and fine motor output.
Babbling	Babbling is a stage in child language acquisition, during which an infant appears to be experimenting with making the sounds of language, but not yet producing any recognizable words.
Lobes	The four major sections of the cerebral cortex: frontal, parietal, temporal, and occipital are called lobes.
Social referencing	Social referencing refers to the process by which infants use the nonverbal emotional expressions of a caregiver as cues to guide their behavior.
Object permanence	Object permanence is the term used to describe the awareness that objects continue to exist even when they are no longer visible. According to Piaget, object permance for the infant develops once the sensorimotor stage is complete.
Problem solving	An attempt to find an appropriate way of attaining a goal when the goal is not readily available is called problem solving.
Pretend play	According to Piaget and Smilansky, pretend play is the third cognitive level of play. It involves imaginary people or situations.

Mutual regulation	Mutual regulation is the process by which infant and caregiver communicate emotional states to each other and respond appropriately.
Postnatal	Postnatal is the period beginning immediately after the birth of a child and extending for about six weeks. The period is also known as postpartum and, less commonly, puerperium.
Society	The social sciences use the term society to mean a group of people that form a semi-closed (or semi-open) social system, in which most interactions are with other individuals belonging to the group.
Pitch	Pitch is the psychological interpretation of a sound or musical tone corresponding to its physical frequency
Prenatal	Prenatal period refers to the time from conception to birth.
Adaptation	Adaptation is a lowering of sensitivity to a stimulus following prolonged exposure to that stimulus. Behavioral adaptations are special ways a particular organism behaves to survive in its natural habitat.
Evolution	Commonly used to refer to gradual change, evolution is the change in the frequency of alleles within a population from one generation to the next. This change may be caused by different mechanisms, including natural selection, genetic drift, or changes in population (gene flow).
Nervous system	The body's electrochemical communication circuitry, made up of billions of neurons is a nervous system.
Neuron	The neuron is the primary cell of the nervous system. They are found in the brain, the spinal cord, in the nerves and ganglia of the peripheral nervous system. It is a specialized cell that conducts impulses through the nervous system and contains three major parts: cell body, dendrites, and an axon. It can have many dendrites but only one axon.
Brain	The brain controls and coordinates most movement, behavior and homeostatic body functions such as heartbeat, blood pressure, fluid balance and body temperature. Functions of the brain are responsible for cognition, emotion, memory, motor learning and other sorts of learning. The brain is primarily made up of two types of cells: glia and neurons.
Central nervous system	The vertebrate central nervous system consists of the brain and spinal cord.
Cowan	Cowan regards working memory not as a separate system, but as a part of long-term memory. Representations in working memory are a subset of the representations in long-term memory.
Cerebral cortex	The cerebral cortex is the outermost layer of the cerebrum and has a grey color. It is made up of four lobes and it is involved in many complex brain functions including memory, perceptual awareness, "thinking", language and consciousness. The cerebral cortex receives sensory information from many different sensory organs eg: eyes, ears, etc. and processes the information.
Nerve	A nerve is an enclosed, cable-like bundle of nerve fibers or axons, which includes the glia that ensheath the axons in myelin. Neurons are sometimes called nerve cells, though this term is technically imprecise since many neurons do not form nerves.
Axon terminal	A swelling at the end of an axon that is designed to release a chemical substance onto another neuron, muscle cell, or gland cell is called the axon terminal.
Axon	An axon, or "nerve fiber," is a long slender projection of a nerve cell, or "neuron," which conducts electrical impulses away from the neuron's cell body or soma.
Dendrite	A dendrite is a slender, typically branched projection of a nerve cell, or "neuron," which conducts the electrical stimulation received from other cells to the body or soma of the cell from which it projects. This stimulation arrives through synapses, which typically are

	located near the tips of the dendrites and away from the soma.
Synapse	A synapse is specialized junction through which cells of the nervous system signal to one another and to non-neuronal cells such as muscles or glands.
Neurotransmitter	A neurotransmitter is a chemical that is used to relay, amplify and modulate electrical signals between a neurons and another cell.
Infancy	The developmental period that extends from birth to 18 or 24 months is called infancy.
Adolescence	The period of life bounded by puberty and the assumption of adult responsibilities is adolescence.
Nucleus	In neuroanatomy, a cluster of cell bodies of neurons within the central nervous system is a nucleus.
Nerve impulse	A nerve impulse is a change in the electric potential of a neuron; a wave of depolarization spreads along the neuron and causes the release of a neurotransmitter.
Myelin	Myelin is an electrically insulating fatty layer that surrounds the axons of many neurons, especially those in the peripheral nervous system. The main consequence of a myelin sheath is an increase in the speed at which impulses propagate along the myelinated fiber. The sheath continues to develop throughout childhood.
Cerebellum	The cerebellum is located in the inferior posterior portion of the head (the hindbrain), directly dorsal to the brainstem and pons, inferior to the occipital lobe. The cerebellum is a region of the brain that plays an important role in the integration of sensory perception and fine motor output.
Visual cortex	The visual cortex is the general term applied to both the primary visual cortex and the visual association area. Anatomically, the visual cortex occupies the entire occipital lobe, the inferior temporal lobe (IT), posterior parts of the parietal lobe, and a few small regions in the frontal lobe.
Embryo	A developed zygote that has a rudimentary heart, brain, and other organs is referred to as an embryo.
Learning	Learning is a relatively permanent change in behavior that results from experience. Thus, to attribute a behavioral change to learning, the change must be relatively permanent and must result from experience.
Species	Species refers to a reproductively isolated breeding population.
Spinal cord	The spinal cord is a part of the vertebrate nervous system that is enclosed in and protected by the vertebral column (it passes through the spinal canal). It consists of nerve cells. The spinal cord carries sensory signals and motor innervation to most of the skeletal muscles in the body.
Brain stem	The brain stem is the stalk of the brain below the cerebral hemispheres. It is the major route for communication between the forebrain and the spinal cord and peripheral nerves. It also controls various functions including respiration, regulation of heart rhythms, and primary aspects of sound localization.
Spinal nerve	The term spinal nerve generally refers to the mixed spinal nerve, which is formed from the dorsal and ventral roots that come out of the spinal cord. The spinal nerve passes out of the vertebrae through the intervertebral foramen.
Stages	Stages represent relatively discrete periods of time in which functioning is qualitatively different from functioning at other periods.
Lobes	The four major sections of the cerebral cortex: frontal, parietal, temporal, and occipital

are called lobes.

Primary motor area	The primary motor area is a group of networked cells that controls movements of specific body parts associated with cell groups in that area of the brain. The area is closely linked by neural networks to corresponding areas in the primary somatosensory cortex.
Primary sensory areas	Primary sensory areas are specialized areas of the cerebral cortex that receive input from sensory nerves and tracts by way of the relay nuclei in the thalamus. They include the visual area, auditory area, and somatosensory area.
Parietal lobe	The parietal lobe is positioned above (superior to) the occipital lobe and behind (posterior to) the frontal lobe. It plays important roles in integrating sensory information from various senses, and in the manipulation of objects.
Receptor	A sensory receptor is a structure that recognizes a stimulus in the internal or external environment of an organism. In response to stimuli the sensory receptor initiates sensory transduction by creating graded potentials or action potentials in the same cell or in an adjacent one.
Sensory receptor	A sensory receptor is a structure that recognizes a stimulus in the environment of an organism. In response to stimuli the sensory receptor initiates sensory transduction by creating graded potentials or action potentials in the same cell or in an adjacent one.
Occipital lobe	The occipital lobe is the smallest of four true lobes in the human brain. Located in the rearmost portion of the skull, the occipital lobe is part of the forebrain structure. It is the visual processing center.
Temporal lobe	The temporal lobe is part of the cerebrum. It lies at the side of the brain, beneath the lateral or Sylvian fissure. Adjacent areas in the superior, posterior and lateral parts of the temporal lobe are involved in high-level auditory processing.
Frontal lobe	The frontal lobe comprises four major folds of cortical tissue: the precentral gyrus, superior gyrus and the middle gyrus of the frontal gyri, the inferior frontal gyrus. It has been found to play a part in impulse control, judgement, language, memory, motor function, problem solving, sexual behavior, socialization and spontaneity.
Perception	Perception is the process of acquiring, interpreting, selecting, and organizing sensory information.
Stimulus	A change in an environmental condition that elicits a response is a stimulus.
Brain circuits	Neurotransmitter currents or neural pathways in the brain are referred to as brain circuits.
Myelination	The process in which the nerve cells are covered and insulated with a layer of fat cells, which increases the speed at which information travels through the nervous system is referred to as myelination.
Neural impulse	Neural impulse refers to the electrochemical discharge of a nerve cell, or neuron.
William James	Functionalism as a psychology developed out of Pragmatism as a philosophy: To find the meaning of an idea, you have to look at its consequences. This led William James and his students towards an emphasis on cause and effect, prediction and control, and observation of environment and behavior, over the careful introspection of the Structuralists.
Maturation	The orderly unfolding of traits, as regulated by the genetic code is called maturation.
Attention	Attention is the cognitive process of selectively concentrating on one thing while ignoring other things. Psychologists have labeled three types of attention: sustained attention, selective attention, and divided attention.
Overt behavior	An action or response that is directly observable and measurable is an overt behavior.

Habituation	In habituation there is a progressive reduction in the response probability with continued repetition of a stimulus.
Phoneme	In oral language, a phoneme is the theoretical basic unit of sound that can be used to distinguish words or morphemes; in sign language, it is a similarly basic unit of hand shape, motion, position, or facial expression.
Baseline	Measure of a particular behavior or process taken before the introduction of the independent variable or treatment is called the baseline.
Control group	A group that does not receive the treatment effect in an experiment is referred to as the control group or sometimes as the comparison group.
Retina	The retina is a thin layer of cells at the back of the eyeball. It is the part of the eye which converts light into nervous signals. The retina contains photoreceptor cells which receive the light; the resulting neural signals then undergo complex processing by other neurons of the retina, and are transformed into action potentials in retinal ganglion cells whose axons form the optic nerve.
Visual acuity	Visual acuity is the eye's ability to detect fine details and is the quantitative measure of the eye's ability to see an in-focus image at a certain distance.
Looking chamber	Fantz's looking chamber was an experimental apparatus used to test infant perception by presenting visual stimuli and observing the infant's responses.
Nearsightedness	A vision deficiency in which close objects are seen clearly but distant objects appear blurry is nearsightedness.
Brightness	The dimension of visual sensation that is dependent on the intensity of light reflected from a surface and that corresponds to the amplitude of the light wave is called brightness.
Rods	Rods are cylindrical shaped photoreceptors that are sensitive to the intensity of light. Rods require less light to function than cone cells, and therefore are the primary source of visual information at night.
Fixation	Fixation in abnormal psychology is the state where an individual becomes obsessed with an attachment to another human, animal or inanimate object. Fixation in vision refers to maintaining the gaze in a constant direction. .
Schematic representation	The representation of objects in terms of real or potential interactions with other objects is called a schematic representation.
Innate	Innate behavior is not learned or influenced by the environment, rather, it is present or predisposed at birth.
Reflex	A simple, involuntary response to a stimulus is referred to as reflex. Reflex actions originate at the spinal cord rather than the brain.
Amniotic fluid	Amniotic fluid refers to fluid within the amniotic sac that suspends and protects the fetus.
Senses	The senses are systems that consist of a sensory cell type that respond to a specific kind of physical energy, and that correspond to a defined region within the brain where the signals are received and interpreted.
Grasping reflex	The grasping reflex is a neonatal reflex that occurs when something touches the infant's palms. The infant responds by grasping tightly.
Moro reflex	Moro reflex refers to a neonatal startle response that occurs in reaction to a sudden, intense noise or movement. When startled, the newborn arches its back, throws its head back, and flings out its arms and legs. The primary significance of this reflex is in evaluating integration of the central nervous system (CNS).

Bowlby	Bowlby, a developmental psychologist of the psychoanalytic tradition, was responsible for much of the early research conducted on attachment in humans. He identified three stages of separation: protest, despair, and detachment.
Stepping reflex	The stepping reflex is where infants take steps when held under the arms and leaned forward so that the feet press against the ground.
Suppression	Suppression is the defense mechanism where a memory is deliberately forgotten.
Piaget	Piaget argued that young children's answers were qualitatively different than older children rather than quantitative. There are two major aspects to his theory: the process of coming to know and the stages we move through as we gradually acquire this ability.
Feedback	Feedback refers to information returned to a person about the effects a response has had.
Rooting reflex	The rooting reflex is a newborn's built-in reaction that occurs when the infant's cheek is stroked or the side of the mouth is touched. In response, the infant turns its head toward the side that was touched in an apparent effort to find something to suck.
Intermodal perception	The ability to relate and integrate information about two or more sensory modalities, such as vision and hearing, is referred to as intermodal perception.
Emotion	An emotion is a mental states that arise spontaneously, rather than through conscious effort. They are often accompanied by physiological changes.
Habit	A habit is a response that has become completely separated from its eliciting stimulus. Early learning theorists used the term to describe S-R associations, however not all S-R associations become a habit, rather many are extinguished after reinforcement is withdrawn.
Primary emotions	Primary emotions, according to Robert Plutchik's theory, are the most basic emotions which include fear, surprise, sadness, disgust, anger, anticipation, joy, and acceptance. Each has high survival value.
Basic emotions	Basic emotions are those found in all cultures, as evidinced by the same facial expressions. They include: fear, anger, disgust, surprise, happiness, and distress.
Ekman	Ekman found that at least some facial expressions and their corresponding emotions are not culturally determined, and thus presumably biological in origin. Expressions he found to be universal included anger, disgust, fear, joy, sadness and surprise.
Guilt	Guilt describes many concepts related to a negative emotion or condition caused by actions which are believed to be, morally wrong. According to Freud, the avoidance of guilt is the basis for moral behavior.
Predisposition	Predisposition refers to an inclination or diathesis to respond in a certain way, either inborn or acquired. In abnormal psychology, it is a factor that lowers the ability to withstand stress and inclines the individual toward pathology.
Human nature	Human nature is the fundamental nature and substance of humans, as well as the range of human behavior that is believed to be invariant over long periods of time and across very different cultural contexts.
Temperament	Temperament refers to a basic, innate disposition to change behavior. The activity level is an important dimension of temperament.
Intuition	Quick, impulsive thought that does not make use of formal logic or clear reasoning is referred to as intuition.
Kagan	The work of Kagan supports the concept of an inborn, biologically based temperamental predisposition to severe anxiety.
Mental	Mental retardation refers to having significantly below-average intellectual functioning and

retardation	limitations in at least two areas of adaptive functioning. Many categorize retardation as mild, moderate, severe, or profound.
Longitudinal study	Longitudinal study is a type of developmental study in which the same group of participants is followed and measured for an extended period of time, often years.
Rubric	In education, a rubric is a set of criteria and standards linked to learning objectives that is used to assess a student's performance on a paper, project, essay, etc.
Trait	An enduring personality characteristic that tends to lead to certain behaviors is called a trait. The term trait also means a genetically inherited feature of an organism.
Tics	Tics are a repeated, impulsive action, almost reflexive in nature, which the person feels powerless to control or avoid.
Arousal	Arousal is a physiological and psychological state involving the activation of the reticular activating system in the brain stem, the autonomic nervous system and the endocrine system, leading to increased heart rate and blood pressure and a condition of alertness and readiness to respond.
Interdependence	Interdependence is a dynamic of being mutually responsible to and dependent on others.
Questionnaire	A self-report method of data collection or clinical assessment method in which the individual being studied checks off items on a printed list, answers multiple-choice questions, or writes out answers to essay questions aimed at producing a selfdescription is called questionnaire.
Deep sleep	Deep sleep refers to stage 4 sleep; the deepest form of normal sleep.
Variable	A variable refers to a measurable factor, characteristic, or attribute of an individual or a system.
Rem sleep	Sleep characterized by rapid eye movements, paralysis of large muscles, fast and irregular heart rate and respiration rate, increased brain-wave activity, and vivid dreams is referred to as REM sleep. An infant spends about half the time in REM sleep when sleeping.
Sleep patterns	The order and timing of daily sleep and waking periods are called sleep patterns.
Physiology	The study of the functions and activities of living cells, tissues, and organs and of the physical and chemical phenomena involved is referred to as physiology.
Anxiety	Anxiety is a complex combination of the feeling of fear, apprehension and worry often accompanied by physical sensations such as palpitations, chest pain and/or shortness of breath.
Sucking reflex	The sucking reflex is a newborn's built-in reaction of automatically sucking an object placed in its mouth. The sucking reflex enables the infant to get nourishment before it has associated a nipple with food.
Qualitative change	A qualitative change refers to a change in kind, structure, or organization, such as the change from nonverbal to verbal communication.
Acquisition	Acquisition is the process of adapting to the environment, learning or becoming conditioned. In classical conditoning terms, it is the initial learning of the stimulus response link, which involves a neutral stimulus being associated with a unconditioned stimulus and becoming a conditioned stimulus.
Conditioning	Conditioning describes the process by which behaviors can be learned or modified through interaction with the environment.
Classical conditioning	Classical conditioning is a simple form of learning in which an organism comes to associate or anticipate events. A neutral stimulus comes to evoke the response usually evoked by a

	natural or unconditioned stimulus by being paired repeatedly with the unconditioned stimulus.
Operant Conditioning	A simple form of learning in which an organism learns to engage in behavior because it is reinforced is referred to as operant conditioning. The consequences of a behavior produce changes in the probability of the behavior's occurence.
Pavlov	Pavlov first described the phenomenon now known as classical conditioning in experiments with dogs.
Graham	Graham has conducted a number of studies that reveal stronger socioeconomic-status influences rather than ethnic influences in achievement.
Theories	Theories are logically self-consistent models or frameworks describing the behavior of a certain natural or social phenomenon. They are broad explanations and predictions concerning phenomena of interest.
Conditional stimulus	A conditional stimulus in a conditional reflex elicits a conditional response.
Conditional response	A conditional response is elicited by a conditional stimulus in a conditional reflex.
Conditioned reflex	The conditioned reflex was Pavlov's term for the conditioned response which is a an acquired response that is under the control of (conditional on the occurrence of) a stimulus
Reinforcement	In operant conditioning, reinforcement is any change in an environment that (a) occurs after the behavior, (b) seems to make that behavior re-occur more often in the future and (c) that reoccurence of behavior must be the result of the change.
Punishment	Punishment is the addtion of a stimulus that reduces the frequency of a response, or the removal of a stimulus that results in a reduction of the response.
Skinner	Skinner conducted research on shaping behavior through positive and negative reinforcement, and demonstrated operant conditioning, a technique which he developed in contrast with classical conditioning.
Positive reinforcement	In positive reinforcement, a stimulus is added and the rate of responding increases.
Reinforcer	In operant conditioning, a reinforcer is any stimulus that increases the probability that a preceding behavior will occur again. In Classical Conditioning, the unconditioned stimulus (US) is the reinforcer.
Operant learning	A simple form of learning in which an organism learns to engage in behavior because it is reinforced is referred to as operant learning. The consequences of a behavior produce changes in the probability of the behavior's occurence.
Individual differences	Individual differences psychology studies the ways in which individual people differ in their behavior. This is distinguished from other aspects of psychology in that although psychology is ostensibly a study of individuals, modern psychologists invariably study groups.
Developmental psychologist	A psychologist interested in human growth and development from conception until death is referred to as a developmental psychologist.
Logical thought	Drawing conclusions on the basis of formal principles of reasoning is referred to as logical thought.
Schema	Schema refers to a way of mentally representing the world, such as a belief or an expectation, that can influence perception of persons, objects, and situations.
Accommodation	Piaget's developmental process of accommodation is the modification of currently held schemes or new schemes so that new information inconsistent with the existing schemes can be

integrated and understood.

Assimilation	According to Piaget, assimilation is the process of the organism interacting with the environment given the organism's cognitive structure. Assimilation is reuse of schemas to fit new information.
Equilibration	Equilibration is a mechanism in Piaget's theory that explains how children or adolescents shift from one state of thought to the next. The shift occurs as they experience cognitive conflict or disequilibrium in trying to understand the world. It is an innate drive to organize experiences to ensure maximal adaptation.
Early childhood	Early childhood refers to the developmental period extending from the end of infancy to about 5 or 6 years of age; sometimes called the preschool years.
Coordination of Secondary Circular Reactions	The fourth stage of sensorimotor development, Coordination of Secondary Circular Reactions, occurs from nine to twelve months, and involves the development of logic; the coordination between means and ends. This is an extremely important stage of development, holding what Piaget calls the "first proper intelligence".
Secondary Circular Reactions	The third stage of Piaget's sensorimotor substages, Secondary Circular Reactions, occurs from four to nine months. The critical requirement for the infant to progress into this substage is hand-eye coordination. Three novelties occur at this stage: intentional grasping for a desired object, repetition of an action involving an external object, and differentiations between ends and means.
Tertiary Circular Reactions	Stage five of the sensorimotor substages, Tertiary Circular Reactions, lasts from twelve to eighteen months, and involves the discovery of new means to meet goals. Piaget describes the child at this juncture as the "young scientist."
Primary circular reaction	A primary circular reaction is a scheme based on the attempt to reproduce an event that initially occurred by chance.
Problem solving	An attempt to find an appropriate way of attaining a goal when the goal is not readily available is called problem solving.
Sensorimotor	The first of Piaget's stages is the Sensorimotor stage. This stage typically ranges from birth to 2 years. In this stage, children experience the world through their senses. During this stage, object permanence and stranger anxiety develop.
Circular reaction	A Circular reaction is Piaget's term for processes by which an infant learns to reproduce desired occurrences originally discovered by chance.
Tactile	Pertaining to the sense of touch is referred to as tactile.
Cognitive development	The process by which a child's understanding of the world changes as a function of age and experience is called cognitive development.
Sensation	Sensation is the first stage in the chain of biochemical and neurologic events that begins with the impinging of a stimulus upon the receptor cells of a sensory organ, which then leads to perception, the mental state that is reflected in statements like "I see a uniformly blue wall."
Shaping	The concept of reinforcing successive, increasingly accurate approximations to a target behavior is called shaping. The target behavior is broken down into a hierarchy of elemental steps, each step more sophisticated then the last. By successively reinforcing each of the the elemental steps, a form of differential reinforcement, until that step is learned while extinguishing the step below, the target behavior is gradually achieved.
Protein	A protein is a complex, high-molecular-weight organic compound that consists of amino acids

joined by peptide bonds. It is essential to the structure and function of all living cells and viruses. Many are enzymes or subunits of enzymes.

Connectedness   Connectedness, according to Cooper, consists of two dimensions: mutuality and permeability. Connectedness involves processes that link the self to others, as seen in acknowledgment of, respect for, and responsiveness to others.

Reciprocity   Reciprocity, in interpersonal attraction, is the tendency to return feelings and attitudes that are expressed about us.

Feedback loop   A system in which the hypothalamus, pituitary gland, and gonads regulate each other's functioning through a series of hormonal messages is a feedback loop.

Go to **Cram101.com** for the Practice Tests for this Chapter.

Perception	Perception is the process of acquiring, interpreting, selecting, and organizing sensory information.
Bruner	Bruner has had an enormous impact on educational psychology with his contributions to cognitive learning theory. His ideas are based on categorization, maintaining that people interpret the world in terms of its similarities and differences.
Brain	The brain controls and coordinates most movement, behavior and homeostatic body functions such as heartbeat, blood pressure, fluid balance and body temperature. Functions of the brain are responsible for cognition, emotion, memory, motor learning and other sorts of learning. The brain is primarily made up of two types of cells: glia and neurons.
Attention	Attention is the cognitive process of selectively concentrating on one thing while ignoring other things. Psychologists have labeled three types of attention: sustained attention, selective attention, and divided attention.
Infancy	The developmental period that extends from birth to 18 or 24 months is called infancy.
Cerebral cortex	The cerebral cortex is the outermost layer of the cerebrum and has a grey color. It is made up of four lobes and it is involved in many complex brain functions including memory, perceptual awareness, "thinking", language and consciousness. The cerebral cortex receives sensory information from many different sensory organs eg: eyes, ears, etc. and processes the information.
Nervous system	The body's electrochemical communication circuitry, made up of billions of neurons is a nervous system.
Maturation	The orderly unfolding of traits, as regulated by the genetic code is called maturation.
Central nervous system	The vertebrate central nervous system consists of the brain and spinal cord.
Emotion	An emotion is a mental states that arise spontaneously, rather than through conscious effort. They are often accompanied by physiological changes.
Adolescence	The period of life bounded by puberty and the assumption of adult responsibilities is adolescence.
Malnutrition	Malnutrition is a general term for the medical condition in a person or animal caused by an unbalanced diet—either too little or too much food, or a diet missing one or more important nutrients.
Chronic	Chronic refers to a relatively long duration, usually more than a few months.
Stages	Stages represent relatively discrete periods of time in which functioning is qualitatively different from functioning at other periods.
Fetal period	The prenatal period of development that begins 2 months after conception and lasts for 7 months, on the average is called the fetal period.
Synaptic density	Synaptic density is believed to be an important indication of the extent of connectivity between neurons.
Wisdom	Wisdom is the ability to make correct judgments and decisions. It is an intangible quality gained through experience. Whether or not something is wise is determined in a pragmatic sense by its popularity, how long it has been around, and its ability to predict against future events.
Prenatal	Prenatal period refers to the time from conception to birth.
Puberty	Puberty refers to the process of physical changes by which a child's body becomes an adult body capable of reproduction.

Go to **Cram101.com** for the Practice Tests for this Chapter.

Synapse	A synapse is specialized junction through which cells of the nervous system signal to one another and to non-neuronal cells such as muscles or glands.
Visual cortex	The visual cortex is the general term applied to both the primary visual cortex and the visual association area. Anatomically, the visual cortex occupies the entire occipital lobe, the inferior temporal lobe (IT), posterior parts of the parietal lobe, and a few small regions in the frontal lobe.
Motor cortex	Motor cortex refers to the section of cortex that lies in the frontal lobe, just across the central fissure from the sensory cortex. Neural impulses in the motor cortex are linked to muscular responses throughout the body.
Individual differences	Individual differences psychology studies the ways in which individual people differ in their behavior. This is distinguished from other aspects of psychology in that although psychology is ostensibly a study of individuals, modern psychologists invariably study groups.
Reflex	A simple, involuntary response to a stimulus is referred to as reflex. Reflex actions originate at the spinal cord rather than the brain.
Eleanor Gibson	Eleanor Gibson contribution to psychology has been her research on the way children learn to perceive their environment. She is remembered for her "visual cliff" experiment which showed how an infant's depth perception helps prevent injuries and falls.
Postnatal	Postnatal is the period beginning immediately after the birth of a child and extending for about six weeks. The period is also known as postpartum and, less commonly, puerperium.
Illusion	An illusion is a distortion of a sensory perception.
Visual cliff	An apparatus used to test depth perception in infants and young animals is the visual cliff. Infants, 6-14 months, were placed on the edge of the visual cliff, a small cliff with a drop-off covered by glass, to see if they would crawl over the edge. Most infants refused to crawl out on the glass signifying that they could perceive depth and that depth perception is not learned.
Experimental group	Experimental group refers to any group receiving a treatment effect in an experiment.
Control group	A group that does not receive the treatment effect in an experiment is referred to as the control group or sometimes as the comparison group.
Hypothesis	A specific statement about behavior or mental processes that is testable through research is a hypothesis.
Affect	A subjective feeling or emotional tone often accompanied by bodily expressions noticeable to others is called affect.
Nurture	Nurture refers to the environmental influences on behavior due to nutrition, culture, socioeconomic status, and learning.
Learning	Learning is a relatively permanent change in behavior that results from experience. Thus, to attribute a behavioral change to learning, the change must be relatively permanent and must result from experience.
Norms	In testing, standards of test performance that permit the comparison of one person's score on the test to the scores of others who have taken the same test are referred to as norms.
Gross motor skills	Gross motor skills refer to motor skills that involve large muscle activities, such as walking.
Sensorimotor	The first of Piaget's stages is the Sensorimotor stage. This stage typically ranges from birth to 2 years. In this stage, children experience the world through their senses. During

	this stage, object permanence and stranger anxiety develop.
Piaget	Piaget argued that young children's answers were qualitatively different than older children rather than quantitative. There are two major aspects to his theory: the process of coming to know and the stages we move through as we gradually acquire this ability.
Qualitative change	A qualitative change refers to a change in kind, structure, or organization, such as the change from nonverbal to verbal communication.
Representati-nal ability	The child's representational ability in Piaget's theory is the capacity to store mental images or symbols of objects and events.
Schema	Schema refers to a way of mentally representing the world, such as a belief or an expectation, that can influence perception of persons, objects, and situations.
Circular reaction	A Circular reaction is Piaget's term for processes by which an infant learns to reproduce desired occurrences originally discovered by chance.
Secondary Circular Reactions	The third stage of Piaget's sensorimotor substages, Secondary Circular Reactions, occurs from four to nine months. The critical requirement for the infant to progress into this substage is hand-eye coordination. Three novelties occur at this stage: intentional grasping for a desired object, repetition of an action involving an external object, and differentiations between ends and means.
Tertiary Circular Reactions	Stage five of the sensorimotor substages, Tertiary Circular Reactions, lasts from twelve to eighteen months, and involves the discovery of new means to meet goals. Piaget describes the child at this juncture as the "young scientist."
Problem solving	An attempt to find an appropriate way of attaining a goal when the goal is not readily available is called problem solving.
Feedback	Feedback refers to information returned to a person about the effects a response has had.
Primary circular reaction	A primary circular reaction is a scheme based on the attempt to reproduce an event that initially occurred by chance.
Intentionality	Brentano defined intentionality as the main characteristic of "psychical phenomena," by which they could be distinguished from "physical phenomena.". Every mental phenomenon, every psychological act has a content, is directed at an object (the intentional object).
Object permanence	Object permanence is the term used to describe the awareness that objects continue to exist even when they are no longer visible. According to Piaget, object permance for the infant develops once the sensorimotor stage is complete.
Society	The social sciences use the term society to mean a group of people that form a semi-closed (or semi-open) social system, in which most interactions are with other individuals belonging to the group.
Perseveration	The persistent repetition of words and ideas, often found in schizophrenia is called perseveration.
Habit	A habit is a response that has become completely separated from its eliciting stimulus. Early learning theorists used the term to describe S-R associations, however not all S-R associations become a habit, rather many are extinguished after reinforcement is withdrawn.
Theories	Theories are logically self-consistent models or frameworks describing the behavior of a certain natural or social phenomenon. They are broad explanations and predictions concerning phenomena of interest.
Habituation	In habituation there is a progressive reduction in the response probability with continued

	repetition of a stimulus.
Scientific research	Research that is objective, systematic, and testable is called scientific research.
Variable	A variable refers to a measurable factor, characteristic, or attribute of an individual or a system.
Causation	Causation concerns the time order relationship between two or more objects such that if a specific antecendent condition occurs the same consequent must always follow.
Innate	Innate behavior is not learned or influenced by the environment, rather, it is present or predisposed at birth.
Cognitive development	The process by which a child's understanding of the world changes as a function of age and experience is called cognitive development.
Inference	Inference is the act or process of drawing a conclusion based solely on what one already knows.
Intuition	Quick, impulsive thought that does not make use of formal logic or clear reasoning is referred to as intuition.
Frontal lobe	The frontal lobe comprises four major folds of cortical tissue: the precentral gyrus, superior gyrus and the middle gyrus of the frontal gyri, the inferior frontal gyrus. It has been found to play a part in impulse control, judgement, language, memory, motor function, problem solving, sexual behavior, socialization and spontaneity.
Lobes	The four major sections of the cerebral cortex: frontal, parietal, temporal, and occipital are called lobes.
Myelin	Myelin is an electrically insulating fatty layer that surrounds the axons of many neurons, especially those in the peripheral nervous system. The main consequence of a myelin sheath is an increase in the speed at which impulses propagate along the myelinated fiber. The sheath continues to develop throughout childhood.
Attachment	Attachment is the tendency to seek closeness to another person and feel secure when that person is present.
Acquisition	Acquisition is the process of adapting to the environment, learning or becoming conditioned. In classical conditoning terms, it is the initial learning of the stimulus response link, which involves a neutral stimulus being associated with a unconditioned stimulus and becoming a conditioned stimulus.
Species	Species refers to a reproductively isolated breeding population.
Explicit memory	Intentional or conscious recollection of information is referred to as explicit memory. Children under age three are usually poorest at explicit memory which may be due to the immaturity of the prefrontal lobes of the brain, which are believed to play an important role in memory for events.
Implicit memory	Implicit memory is the long-term memory of skills and procedures, or "how to" knowledge. It is often not easily verbalized, but can be used without consciously thinking about it.
Senses	The senses are systems that consist of a sensory cell type that respond to a specific kind of physical energy, and that correspond to a defined region within the brain where the signals are received and interpreted.
Mental Representation	Stage six of the sensorimotor substages, Mental representation, 18 months to 2 years, marks the beginnings of insight, or true creativity. This marks the passage into unique thought in Piaget's later three areas of development.

Go to Cram101.com for the Practice Tests for this Chapter.

Deferred imitation	Imitation that occurs after a time delay of hours or days is referred to as deferred imitation.
Developmental psychologist	A psychologist interested in human growth and development from conception until death is referred to as a developmental psychologist.
Rote	Rote learning, is a learning technique which avoids grasping the inner complexities and inferences of the subject that is being learned and instead focuses on memorizing the material so that it can be recalled by the learner exactly the way it was read or heard.
Zone of proximal development	The zone of proximal development is the gap between a learner's current or actual level of development determined by independent problem solving and the learner's emerging or potential level of development. Learners cannot build new knowledge without first having a framework or prior learning foundation.
Proximal	Students can set both long-term (distal) and short-term (proximal) goals .
Vygotsky	The Vygotsky model of human development has been termed as a sociocultural approach. The individual's development is a result of his or her culture.
Empirical	Empirical means the use of working hypotheses which are capable of being disproved using observation or experiment.
Primary caregiver	Primary caregiver refers to a person primarily responsible for the care of an infant, usually the infant's mother or father.
Social referencing	Social referencing refers to the process by which infants use the nonverbal emotional expressions of a caregiver as cues to guide their behavior.
Cooing	Cooing is the spontaneous repetition of vowel sounds by infants.
Left hemisphere	The left hemisphere of the cortex controls the right side of the body, coordinates complex movements, and, in 95% of people, controls the production of speech and written language.
Babbling	Babbling is a stage in child language acquisition, during which an infant appears to be experimenting with making the sounds of language, but not yet producing any recognizable words.
Intonation	The use of pitches of varying levels to help communicate meaning is called intonation.
Motor neuron	A motor neuron is an efferent neuron that originates in the spinal cord and synapses with muscle fibers to facilitate muscle contraction and with muscle spindles to modify proprioceptive sensitivity.
Hippocampus	The hippocampus is a part of the brain located inside the temporal lobe. It forms a part of the limbic system and plays a part in memory and navigation.
Myelination	The process in which the nerve cells are covered and insulated with a layer of fat cells, which increases the speed at which information travels through the nervous system is referred to as myelination.
Cerebellum	The cerebellum is located in the inferior posterior portion of the head (the hindbrain), directly dorsal to the brainstem and pons, inferior to the occipital lobe. The cerebellum is a region of the brain that plays an important role in the integration of sensory perception and fine motor output.
Neuron	The neuron is the primary cell of the nervous system. They are found in the brain, the spinal cord, in the nerves and ganglia of the peripheral nervous system. It is a specialized cell that conducts impulses through the nervous system and contains three major parts: cell body, dendrites, and an axon. It can have many dendrites but only one axon.
Adaptation	Adaptation is a lowering of sensitivity to a stimulus following prolonged exposure to that

stimulus. Behavioral adaptations are special ways a particular organism behaves to survive in its natural habitat.

Prefrontal cortex	The prefrontal cortex is the anterior part of the frontal lobes of the brain, lying in front of the motor and associative areas. It has been implicated in planning complex cognitive behaviors, personality expression and moderating correct social behavior. The prefrontal cortex continues to develop until around age 6.
Perceptual features	Perceptual features are the interpreted basic elements of a stimulus, such as lines, shapes, edges, or colors.
Cognition	The intellectual processes through which information is obtained, transformed, stored, retrieved, and otherwise used is cognition.
Mutation	Mutation is a permanent, sometimes transmissible (if the change is to a germ cell) change to the genetic material (usually DNA or RNA) of a cell. They can be caused by copying errors in the genetic material during cell division and by exposure to radiation, chemicals, or viruses, or can occur deliberately under cellular control during the processes such as meiosis or hypermutation.

Attention	Attention is the cognitive process of selectively concentrating on one thing while ignoring other things. Psychologists have labeled three types of attention: sustained attention, selective attention, and divided attention.
Infancy	The developmental period that extends from birth to 18 or 24 months is called infancy.
Learning	Learning is a relatively permanent change in behavior that results from experience. Thus, to attribute a behavioral change to learning, the change must be relatively permanent and must result from experience.
Toddler	A toddler is a child between the ages of one and three years old. During this period, the child learns a great deal about social roles and develops motor skills; to toddle is to walk unsteadily.
Pretend play	According to Piaget and Smilansky, pretend play is the third cognitive level of play. It involves imaginary people or situations.
Emotion	An emotion is a mental states that arise spontaneously, rather than through conscious effort. They are often accompanied by physiological changes.
Maturation	The orderly unfolding of traits, as regulated by the genetic code is called maturation.
Cerebral cortex	The cerebral cortex is the outermost layer of the cerebrum and has a grey color. It is made up of four lobes and it is involved in many complex brain functions including memory, perceptual awareness, "thinking", language and consciousness. The cerebral cortex receives sensory information from many different sensory organs eg: eyes, ears, etc. and processes the information.
Nervous system	The body's electrochemical communication circuitry, made up of billions of neurons is a nervous system.
Myelination	The process in which the nerve cells are covered and insulated with a layer of fat cells, which increases the speed at which information travels through the nervous system is referred to as myelination.
Brain stem	The brain stem is the stalk of the brain below the cerebral hemispheres. It is the major route for communication between the forebrain and the spinal cord and peripheral nerves. It also controls various functions including respiration, regulation of heart rhythms, and primary aspects of sound localization.
Neuron	The neuron is the primary cell of the nervous system. They are found in the brain, the spinal cord, in the nerves and ganglia of the peripheral nervous system. It is a specialized cell that conducts impulses through the nervous system and contains three major parts: cell body, dendrites, and an axon. It can have many dendrites but only one axon.
Brain	The brain controls and coordinates most movement, behavior and homeostatic body functions such as heartbeat, blood pressure, fluid balance and body temperature. Functions of the brain are responsible for cognition, emotion, memory, motor learning and other sorts of learning. The brain is primarily made up of two types of cells: glia and neurons.
Central nervous system	The vertebrate central nervous system consists of the brain and spinal cord.
Perception	Perception is the process of acquiring, interpreting, selecting, and organizing sensory information.
Fisher	Fisher was a eugenicist, evolutionary biologist, geneticist and statistician. He has been described as "The greatest of Darwin's successors", and a genius who almost single-handedly created the foundations for modern statistical science inventing the techniques of maximum likelihood and analysis of variance.

Qualitative change	A qualitative change refers to a change in kind, structure, or organization, such as the change from nonverbal to verbal communication.
Sensorimotor	The first of Piaget's stages is the Sensorimotor stage. This stage typically ranges from birth to 2 years. In this stage, children experience the world through their senses. During this stage, object permanence and stranger anxiety develop.
Tertiary Circular Reactions	Stage five of the sensorimotor substages, Tertiary Circular Reactions, lasts from twelve to eighteen months, and involves the discovery of new means to meet goals. Piaget describes the child at this juncture as the "young scientist."
Piaget	Piaget argued that young children's answers were qualitatively different than older children rather than quantitative. There are two major aspects to his theory: the process of coming to know and the stages we move through as we gradually acquire this ability.
Circular reaction	A Circular reaction is Piaget's term for processes by which an infant learns to reproduce desired occurrences originally discovered by chance.
Secondary Circular Reactions	The third stage of Piaget's sensorimotor substages, Secondary Circular Reactions, occurs from four to nine months. The critical requirement for the infant to progress into this substage is hand-eye coordination. Three novelties occur at this stage: intentional grasping for a desired object, repetition of an action involving an external object, and differentiations between ends and means.
Problem solving	An attempt to find an appropriate way of attaining a goal when the goal is not readily available is called problem solving.
Schema	Schema refers to a way of mentally representing the world, such as a belief or an expectation, that can influence perception of persons, objects, and situations.
Mental Representation	Stage six of the sensorimotor substages, Mental representation, 18 months to 2 years, marks the beginnings of insight, or true creativity. This marks the passage into unique thought in Piaget's later three areas of development.
Trial and error	Trial and error is an approach to problem solving in which one solution after another is tried in no particular order until an answer is found.
Stages	Stages represent relatively discrete periods of time in which functioning is qualitatively different from functioning at other periods.
Norms	In testing, standards of test performance that permit the comparison of one person's score on the test to the scores of others who have taken the same test are referred to as norms.
Developmental norms	The average age at which individuals display various behaviors and abilities are called developmental norms.
Senses	The senses are systems that consist of a sensory cell type that respond to a specific kind of physical energy, and that correspond to a defined region within the brain where the signals are received and interpreted.
Cognitive development	The process by which a child's understanding of the world changes as a function of age and experience is called cognitive development.
Sensorimotor play	Behavior engaged in by infants that exercises their existing sensorimotor schemas is referred to as sensorimotor play.
Deferred imitation	Imitation that occurs after a time delay of hours or days is referred to as deferred imitation.
Construct	A generalized concept, such as anxiety or gravity, is a construct.
Dual	The ability to represent an object simultaneously as the object itself and as a

representation	representation of something else is referred to as dual representation.
Acquisition	Acquisition is the process of adapting to the environment, learning or becoming conditioned. In classical conditoning terms, it is the initial learning of the stimulus response link, which involves a neutral stimulus being associated with a unconditioned stimulus and becoming a conditioned stimulus.
Attachment	Attachment is the tendency to seek closeness to another person and feel secure when that person is present.
Primary caregiver	Primary caregiver refers to a person primarily responsible for the care of an infant, usually the infant's mother or father.
Sigmund Freud	Sigmund Freud was the founder of the psychoanalytic school, based on his theory that unconscious motives control much behavior, that particular kinds of unconscious thoughts and memories are the source of neurosis, and that neurosis could be treated through bringing these unconscious thoughts and memories to consciousness in psychoanalytic treatment.
Erik Erikson	Erik Erikson conceived eight stages of development, each confronting the individual with its own psychosocial demands, that continued into old age. Personality development, according to Erikson, takes place through a series of crises that must be overcome and internalized by the individual in preparation for the next developmental stage. Such crisis are not catastrophes but vulnerabilities.
Hypothesis	A specific statement about behavior or mental processes that is testable through research is a hypothesis.
Bowlby	Bowlby, a developmental psychologist of the psychoanalytic tradition, was responsible for much of the early research conducted on attachment in humans. He identified three stages of separation: protest, despair, and detachment.
Personality	Personality refers to the pattern of enduring characteristics that differentiates a person, the patterns of behaviors that make each individual unique.
Social development	The person's developing capacity for social relationships and the effects of those relationships on further development is referred to as social development.
Prototype	A concept of a category of objects or events that serves as a good example of the category is called a prototype.
Arousal	Arousal is a physiological and psychological state involving the activation of the reticular activating system in the brain stem, the autonomic nervous system and the endocrine system, leading to increased heart rate and blood pressure and a condition of alertness and readiness to respond.
Psychiatrist	A psychiatrist is a physician who specializes in the diagnosis and treatment of psychological disorders.
Psychodynamic	Most psychodynamic approaches are centered around the idea of a maladapted function developed early in life (usually childhood) which are at least in part unconscious. This maladapted function (a.k.a. defense mechanism) does not do well in place of a normal/healthy one.
Anxiety	Anxiety is a complex combination of the feeling of fear, apprehension and worry often accompanied by physical sensations such as palpitations, chest pain and/or shortness of breath.
Scheme	According to Piaget, a hypothetical mental structure that permits the classification and organization of new information is called a scheme.
Postnatal	Postnatal is the period beginning immediately after the birth of a child and extending for about six weeks. The period is also known as postpartum and, less commonly, puerperium.

Go to **Cram101.com** for the Practice Tests for this Chapter.

Species	Species refers to a reproductively isolated breeding population.
Analogy	An analogy is a comparison between two different things, in order to highlight some form of similarity. Analogy is the cognitive process of transferring information from a particular subject to another particular subject.
Set point	Set point refers to any one of a number of quantities (e.g. body weight, body temperature) which the body tries to keep at a particular value
Separation anxiety	Separation anxiety is a psychological condition in which an individual has excessive anxiety regarding separation from home, or from those with whom the individual has a strong attachment.
Harlow	Harlow and his famous wire and cloth surrogate mother monkey studies demonstrated that the need for affection created a stronger bond between mother and infant than did physical needs. He also found that the more discrimination problems the monkeys solved, the better they became at solving them.
Evolutionary theory	Evolutionary theory is concerned with heritable variability rather than behavioral variations. Natural selection requirements: (1) natural variability within a species must exist, (2) only some individual differences are heritable, and (3) natural selection only takes place when there is an interaction between the inborn attributes of organisms and the environment in which they live.
Fixation	Fixation in abnormal psychology is the state where an individual becomes obsessed with an attachment to another human, animal or inanimate object. Fixation in vision refers to maintaining the gaze in a constant direction. .
Strange situation	An observational measure of infant attachment that requires the infant to move through a series of introductions, separations, and reunions with the caregiver and an adult stranger in a prescribed order is called Ainsworth's strange situation.
Insecure attachment	Insecure attachment occurs when infants either avoid the caregiver or show considerable resistance or ambivalence toward the caregiver.
Secure attachment	With secure attachment, the infant uses a caregiver as a secure base from which to explore the environment. Ainsworth believes that secure attachment in the first year of life provides an important foundation for psychological development later in life.
Society	The social sciences use the term society to mean a group of people that form a semi-closed (or semi-open) social system, in which most interactions are with other individuals belonging to the group.
Positive relationship	Statistically, a positive relationship refers to a mathematical relationship in which increases in one measure are matched by increases in the other.
Antecedents	In behavior modification, events that typically precede the target response are called antecedents.
Synchrony	In child development, synchrony is the carefully coordinated interaction between the parent and the child or adolescent in which, often unknowingly, they are attuned to each other's behavior.
Correlation	A statistical technique for determining the degree of association between two or more variables is referred to as correlation.
Temperament	Temperament refers to a basic, innate disposition to change behavior. The activity level is an important dimension of temperament.
Kagan	The work of Kagan supports the concept of an inborn, biologically based temperamental predisposition to severe anxiety.

Go to **Cram101.com** for the Practice Tests for this Chapter.

Developmental psychologist	A psychologist interested in human growth and development from conception until death is referred to as a developmental psychologist.
Consciousness	The awareness of the sensations, thoughts, and feelings being experienced at a given moment is called consciousness.
Reflection	Reflection is the process of rephrasing or repeating thoughts and feelings expressed, making the person more aware of what they are saying or thinking.
Guilt	Guilt describes many concepts related to a negative emotion or condition caused by actions which are believed to be, morally wrong. According to Freud, the avoidance of guilt is the basis for moral behavior.
Primary emotions	Primary emotions, according to Robert Plutchik's theory, are the most basic emotions which include fear, surprise, sadness, disgust, anger, anticipation, joy, and acceptance. Each has high survival value.
Early childhood	Early childhood refers to the developmental period extending from the end of infancy to about 5 or 6 years of age; sometimes called the preschool years.
Theories	Theories are logically self-consistent models or frameworks describing the behavior of a certain natural or social phenomenon. They are broad explanations and predictions concerning phenomena of interest.
Sensation	Sensation is the first stage in the chain of biochemical and neurologic events that begins with the impinging of a stimulus upon the receptor cells of a sensory organ, which then leads to perception, the mental state that is reflected in statements like "I see a uniformly blue wall."
Tactile	Pertaining to the sense of touch is referred to as tactile.

Go to **Cram101.com** for the Practice Tests for this Chapter.
And, **NEVER** highlight a book again!

Bronfenbrenner	Bronfenbrenner was a co-founder of the U.S. national Head Start program and founder of the Ecological Theory of Development.
Attachment	Attachment is the tendency to seek closeness to another person and feel secure when that person is present.
Transactional model	Transactional model refers to a framework that views development as the continuous and bidirectional interchange between an active organism with a unique biological constitution, and a changing environment.
Harlow	Harlow and his famous wire and cloth surrogate mother monkey studies demonstrated that the need for affection created a stronger bond between mother and infant than did physical needs. He also found that the more discrimination problems the monkeys solved, the better they became at solving them.
Infancy	The developmental period that extends from birth to 18 or 24 months is called infancy.
Plato	According to Plato, people must come equipped with most of their knowledge and need only hints and contemplation to complete it. Plato suggested that the brain is the mechanism of mental processes and that one gained knowledge by reflecting on the contents of one's mind.
Brazelton	Brazelton Neonatal Behavioral Assessment Scale is a test given several days after birth to assess newborns' neurological development, reflexes, and reactions to people.
Deprivation	Deprivation, is the loss or withholding of normal stimulation, nutrition, comfort, love, and so forth; a condition of lacking. The level of stimulation is less than what is required.
Society	The social sciences use the term society to mean a group of people that form a semi-closed (or semi-open) social system, in which most interactions are with other individuals belonging to the group.
Early childhood	Early childhood refers to the developmental period extending from the end of infancy to about 5 or 6 years of age; sometimes called the preschool years.
Correlation	A statistical technique for determining the degree of association between two or more variables is referred to as correlation.
Causation	Causation concerns the time order relationship between two or more objects such that if a specific antecendent condition occurs the same consequent must always follow.
Temperament	Temperament refers to a basic, innate disposition to change behavior. The activity level is an important dimension of temperament.
Species	Species refers to a reproductively isolated breeding population.
Insight	Insight refers to a sudden awareness of the relationships among various elements that had previously appeared to be independent of one another.
Plasticity	The capacity for modification and change is referred to as plasticity.
Secure attachment	With secure attachment, the infant uses a caregiver as a secure base from which to explore the environment. Ainsworth believes that secure attachment in the first year of life provides an important foundation for psychological development later in life.
Friendship	The essentials of friendship are reciprocity and commitment between individuals who see themselves more or less as equals. Interaction between friends rests on a more equal power base than the interaction between children and adults.
Bowlby	Bowlby, a developmental psychologist of the psychoanalytic tradition, was responsible for much of the early research conducted on attachment in humans. He identified three stages of separation: protest, despair, and detachment.

Primary caregiver	Primary caregiver refers to a person primarily responsible for the care of an infant, usually the infant's mother or father.
Longitudinal study	Longitudinal study is a type of developmental study in which the same group of participants is followed and measured for an extended period of time, often years.
Generalization	In conditioning, the tendency for a conditioned response to be evoked by stimuli that are similar to the stimulus to which the response was conditioned is a generalization. The greater the similarity among the stimuli, the greater the probability of generalization.
Toddler	A toddler is a child between the ages of one and three years old. During this period, the child learns a great deal about social roles and develops motor skills; to toddle is to walk unsteadily.
Ethnicity	Ethnicity refers to a characteristic based on cultural heritage, nationality characteristics, race, religion, and language.
Socioeconomic	Socioeconomic pertains to the study of the social and economic impacts of any product or service offering, market intervention or other activity on an economy as a whole and on the companies, organization and individuals who are its main economic actors.
Socioeconomic Status	A family's socioeconomic status is based on family income, parental education level, parental occupation, and social status in the community. Those with high status often have more success in preparing their children for school because they have access to a wide range of resources.
Affect	A subjective feeling or emotional tone often accompanied by bodily expressions noticeable to others is called affect.
Nurture	Nurture refers to the environmental influences on behavior due to nutrition, culture, socioeconomic status, and learning.
Attention	Attention is the cognitive process of selectively concentrating on one thing while ignoring other things. Psychologists have labeled three types of attention: sustained attention, selective attention, and divided attention.
Standardized test	An oral or written assessment for which an individual receives a score indicating how the individual reponded relative to a previously tested large sample of others is referred to as a standardized test.
Insecure attachment	Insecure attachment occurs when infants either avoid the caregiver or show considerable resistance or ambivalence toward the caregiver.
Strange situation	An observational measure of infant attachment that requires the infant to move through a series of introductions, separations, and reunions with the caregiver and an adult stranger in a prescribed order is called Ainsworth's strange situation.
Prenatal	Prenatal period refers to the time from conception to birth.
Hyperactivity	Hyperactivity can be described as a state in which a individual is abnormally easily excitable and exuberant. Strong emotional reactions and a very short span of attention is also typical for the individual.
Cognitive development	The process by which a child's understanding of the world changes as a function of age and experience is called cognitive development.
Statistics	Statistics is a type of data analysis which practice includes the planning, summarizing, and interpreting of observations of a system possibly followed by predicting or forecasting of future events based on a mathematical model of the system being observed.
Statistic	A statistic is an observable random variable of a sample.

Maladjustment	Maladjustment is the condition of being unable to adapt properly to your environment with resulting emotional instability.
Psychological test	Psychological test refers to a standardized measure of a sample of a person's behavior.
Emotion	An emotion is a mental states that arise spontaneously, rather than through conscious effort. They are often accompanied by physiological changes.
Psychiatrist	A psychiatrist is a physician who specializes in the diagnosis and treatment of psychological disorders.
Theories	Theories are logically self-consistent models or frameworks describing the behavior of a certain natural or social phenomenon. They are broad explanations and predictions concerning phenomena of interest.
Child development	Scientific study of the processes of change from conception through adolescence is called child development.
Critical period	A period of time when an innate response can be elicited by a particular stimulus is referred to as the critical period.
Hypothesis	A specific statement about behavior or mental processes that is testable through research is a hypothesis.
Puberty	Puberty refers to the process of physical changes by which a child's body becomes an adult body capable of reproduction.
Acquisition	Acquisition is the process of adapting to the environment, learning or becoming conditioned. In classical conditoning terms, it is the initial learning of the stimulus response link, which involves a neutral stimulus being associated with a unconditioned stimulus and becoming a conditioned stimulus.
Learning	Learning is a relatively permanent change in behavior that results from experience. Thus, to attribute a behavioral change to learning, the change must be relatively permanent and must result from experience.
Case study	A carefully drawn biography that may be obtained through interviews, questionnaires, and psychological tests is called a case study.
Anecdotal evidence	Anecdotal evidence is unreliable evidence based on personal experience that has not been empirically tested, and which is often used in an argument as if it had been scientifically or statistically proven. The person using anecdotal evidence may or may not be aware of the fact that, by doing so, they are generalizing.
Population	Population refers to all members of a well-defined group of organisms, events, or things.
Individual differences	Individual differences psychology studies the ways in which individual people differ in their behavior. This is distinguished from other aspects of psychology in that although psychology is ostensibly a study of individuals, modern psychologists invariably study groups.
Alcoholic	An alcoholic is dependent on alcohol as characterized by craving, loss of control, physical dependence and withdrawal symptoms, and tolerance.
Protective factors	Protective factors are influences that reduce the impact of early stress and tend to lead to positive outcomes.
Trait	An enduring personality characteristic that tends to lead to certain behaviors is called a trait. The term trait also means a genetically inherited feature of an organism.
Questionnaire	A self-report method of data collection or clinical assessment method in which the individual being studied checks off items on a printed list, answers multiple-choice questions, or

writes out answers to essay questions aimed at producing a selfdescription is called questionnaire.

Personality	Personality refers to the pattern of enduring characteristics that differentiates a person, the patterns of behaviors that make each individual unique.
Personality test	A personality test aims to describe aspects of a person's character that remain stable across situations.
Autonomy	Autonomy is the condition of something that does not depend on anything else.
Psychopathology	Psychopathology refers to the field concerned with the nature and development of mental disorders.
Depression	In everyday language depression refers to any downturn in mood, which may be relatively transitory and perhaps due to something trivial. This is differentiated from Clinical depression which is marked by symptoms that last two weeks or more and are so severe that they interfere with daily living.
Adolescence	The period of life bounded by puberty and the assumption of adult responsibilities is adolescence.
Chronic	Chronic refers to a relatively long duration, usually more than a few months.
Schizophrenia	Schizophrenia is characterized by persistent defects in the perception or expression of reality. A person suffering from untreated schizophrenia typically demonstrates grossly disorganized thinking, and may also experience delusions or auditory hallucinations
Phenotype	The phenotype of an individual organism is either its total physical appearance and constitution, or a specific manifestation of a trait, such as size or eye color, that varies between individuals. Phenotype is determined to some extent by genotype, or by the identity of the alleles that an individual carries at one or more positions on the chromosomes.
Genotype	The genotype is the specific genetic makeup of an individual, usually in the form of DNA. It codes for the phenotype of that individual. Any given gene will usually cause an observable change in an organism, known as the phenotype.
Social support	Social Support is the physical and emotional comfort given by family, friends, co-workers and others. Research has identified three main types of social support: emotional, practical, sharing points of view.
Psychological disorder	Mental processes and/or behavior patterns that cause emotional distress and/or substantial impairment in functioning is a psychological disorder.
Syndrome	The term syndrome is the association of several clinically recognizable features, signs, symptoms, phenomena or characteristics which often occur together, so that the presence of one feature indicates the presence of the others.
Trauma	Trauma refers to a severe physical injury or wound to the body caused by an external force, or a psychological shock having a lasting effect on mental life.
Nightmare	Nightmare was the original term for the state later known as waking dream, and more currently as sleep paralysis, associated with rapid eye movement (REM) periods of sleep.
Anxiety	Anxiety is a complex combination of the feeling of fear, apprehension and worry often accompanied by physical sensations such as palpitations, chest pain and/or shortness of breath.
Separation anxiety	Separation anxiety is a psychological condition in which an individual has excessive anxiety regarding separation from home, or from those with whom the individual has a strong attachment.

Authoritarian	The term authoritarian is used to describe a style that enforces strong and sometimes oppressive measures against those in its sphere of influence, generally without attempts at gaining their consent.
Experimental group	Experimental group refers to any group receiving a treatment effect in an experiment.
Control group	A group that does not receive the treatment effect in an experiment is referred to as the control group or sometimes as the comparison group.
Life satisfaction	A person's attitudes about his or her overall life are referred to as life satisfaction.
Punishment	Punishment is the addtion of a stimulus that reduces the frequency of a response, or the removal of a stimulus that results in a reduction of the response.
Adaptation	Adaptation is a lowering of sensitivity to a stimulus following prolonged exposure to that stimulus. Behavioral adaptations are special ways a particular organism behaves to survive in its natural habitat.
Psychotherapy	Psychotherapy is a set of techniques based on psychological principles intended to improve mental health, emotional or behavioral issues. Commonly psychotherapy involves a therapist and client(s), who discuss their issues in an effort to discover what they are and how they can solve them.
Blocking	If the one of the two members of a compound stimulus fails to produce the CR due to an earlier conditioning of the other member of the compound stimulus, blocking has occurred.
Gender difference	A gender difference is a disparity between genders involving quality or quantity. Though some gender differences are controversial, they are not to be confused with sexist stereotypes.
Social play	Play that involves social interactions with peers is called social play. It increases affiliation with peers, releases tension, advances cognitive development, and increases exploration.
Spontaneous recovery	The recurrence of an extinguished response as a function of the passage of time is referred to as spontaneous recovery.
Social development	The person's developing capacity for social relationships and the effects of those relationships on further development is referred to as social development.
Pathology	Pathology is the study of the processes underlying disease and other forms of illness, harmful abnormality, or dysfunction.
Hartup	According to Hartup, the single best childhood predictor of adult adaptation is not school grades, and not classroom behavior, but rather, the adequacy with which the child gets along with other children.
Shaping	The concept of reinforcing successive, increasingly accurate approximations to a target behavior is called shaping. The target behavior is broken down into a hierarchy of elemental steps, each step more sophisticated then the last. By successively reinforcing each of the the elemental steps, a form of differential reinforcement, until that step is learned while extinguishing the step below, the target behavior is gradually achieved.
Hormone	A hormone is a chemical messenger from one cell (or group of cells) to another. The best known are those produced by endocrine glands, but they are produced by nearly every organ system. The function of hormones is to serve as a signal to the target cells; the action of the hormone is determined by the pattern of secretion and the signal transduction of the receiving tissue.
Cultural values	The importance and desirability of various objects and activities as defined by people in a

	given culture are referred to as cultural values.
Kierkegaard	Kierkegaard has achieved general recognition as the first existentialist philosopher, though some new research shows this may be a more difficult connection than previously thought.
Illusion	An illusion is a distortion of a sensory perception.
Discrimination	In Learning theory, discrimination refers the ability to distinguish between a conditioned stimulus and other stimuli. It can be brought about by extensive training or differential reinforcement. In social terms, it is the denial of privileges to a person or a group on the basis of prejudice.
Stages	Stages represent relatively discrete periods of time in which functioning is qualitatively different from functioning at other periods.
Prejudice	Prejudice in general, implies coming to a judgment on the subject before learning where the preponderance of the evidence actually lies, or formation of a judgement without direct experience.
Moral development	Development regarding rules and conventions about what people should do in their interactions with other people is called moral development.
Parental responsiveness	Parental responsiveness is the degree of caregiving that is based on sensitivity to a child's feelings, needs, rhythms, and signals.
Schematic representation	The representation of objects in terms of real or potential interactions with other objects is called a schematic representation.
Maturation	The orderly unfolding of traits, as regulated by the genetic code is called maturation.
Brain	The brain controls and coordinates most movement, behavior and homeostatic body functions such as heartbeat, blood pressure, fluid balance and body temperature. Functions of the brain are responsible for cognition, emotion, memory, motor learning and other sorts of learning. The brain is primarily made up of two types of cells: glia and neurons.

Early childhood	Early childhood refers to the developmental period extending from the end of infancy to about 5 or 6 years of age; sometimes called the preschool years.
Society	The social sciences use the term society to mean a group of people that form a semi-closed (or semi-open) social system, in which most interactions are with other individuals belonging to the group.
Theories	Theories are logically self-consistent models or frameworks describing the behavior of a certain natural or social phenomenon. They are broad explanations and predictions concerning phenomena of interest.
Phoneme	In oral language, a phoneme is the theoretical basic unit of sound that can be used to distinguish words or morphemes; in sign language, it is a similarly basic unit of hand shape, motion, position, or facial expression.
Babbling	Babbling is a stage in child language acquisition, during which an infant appears to be experimenting with making the sounds of language, but not yet producing any recognizable words.
Cooing	Cooing is the spontaneous repetition of vowel sounds by infants.
Learning	Learning is a relatively permanent change in behavior that results from experience. Thus, to attribute a behavioral change to learning, the change must be relatively permanent and must result from experience.
Social referencing	Social referencing refers to the process by which infants use the nonverbal emotional expressions of a caregiver as cues to guide their behavior.
Acquisition	Acquisition is the process of adapting to the environment, learning or becoming conditioned. In classical conditoning terms, it is the initial learning of the stimulus response link, which involves a neutral stimulus being associated with a unconditioned stimulus and becoming a conditioned stimulus.
Attention	Attention is the cognitive process of selectively concentrating on one thing while ignoring other things. Psychologists have labeled three types of attention: sustained attention, selective attention, and divided attention.
Species	Species refers to a reproductively isolated breeding population.
Intuition	Quick, impulsive thought that does not make use of formal logic or clear reasoning is referred to as intuition.
Chomsky	Chomsky has greatly influenced the field of theoretical linguistics with his work on the theory of generative grammar. Accordingly, humans are biologically prewired to learn language at a certain time and in a certain way.
Morpheme	A morpheme is the smallest language unit that carries a semantic interpretation. They are, generally, a distinctive collocation of phonemes (as the free form pin or the bound form -s of pins) having no smaller meaningful members.
Feedback	Feedback refers to information returned to a person about the effects a response has had.
Norms	In testing, standards of test performance that permit the comparison of one person's score on the test to the scores of others who have taken the same test are referred to as norms.
Toddler	A toddler is a child between the ages of one and three years old. During this period, the child learns a great deal about social roles and develops motor skills; to toddle is to walk unsteadily.
Denial	Denial is a psychological defense mechanism in which a person faced with a fact that is uncomfortable or painful to accept rejects it instead, insisting that it is not true despite

Go to **Cram101.com** for the Practice Tests for this Chapter.

what may be overwhelming evidence.

Overextension

Overgeneralizing the use of words to objects and situations to which they do not apply is overextension. This is a normal characteristic of the speech of young children.

Underextension

Restricting the use of a word to only a few, rather than to all, members of a class of objects is underextension.

Emotion

An emotion is a mental states that arise spontaneously, rather than through conscious effort. They are often accompanied by physiological changes.

Reasoning

Reasoning is the act of using reason to derive a conclusion from certain premises. There are two main methods to reach a conclusion, deductive reasoning and inductive reasoning.

Senses

The senses are systems that consist of a sensory cell type that respond to a specific kind of physical energy, and that correspond to a defined region within the brain where the signals are received and interpreted.

Infancy

The developmental period that extends from birth to 18 or 24 months is called infancy.

Holophrase

A holophrase is a single word expressing a complex idea. Children go through a stage early in life where they are only able to communicate complex ideas using single words. Sometimes the single words can seem to communicate as much as a full sentence would.

Mean length of utterance

Mean length of Utterance is a measure of linguistic productivity in children. It is traditionally calculated by collecting 100 utterances spoken by a child and dividing the number of utterances by the number of morphemes in the corpus. A higher score is taken to indicate a higher level of language proficiency.

Metaphor

A metaphor is a rhetorical trope where a comparison is made between two seemingly unrelated subjects

Nurture

Nurture refers to the environmental influences on behavior due to nutrition, culture, socioeconomic status, and learning.

Nativist

A nativist believes that certain skills or abilities are native or hard wired into the brain at birth.

Conditioning

Conditioning describes the process by which behaviors can be learned or modified through interaction with the environment.

Operant Conditioning

A simple form of learning in which an organism learns to engage in behavior because it is reinforced is referred to as operant conditioning. The consequences of a behavior produce changes in the probability of the behavior's occurence.

Maturation

The orderly unfolding of traits, as regulated by the genetic code is called maturation.

Analogy

An analogy is a comparison between two different things, in order to highlight some form of similarity. Analogy is the cognitive process of transferring information from a particular subject to another particular subject.

Liver

The liver plays a major role in metabolism and has a number of functions in the body including detoxification, glycogen storage and plasma protein synthesis. It also produces bile, which is important for digestion. The liver converts most carbohydrates, proteing, and fats into glucose.

Psycholinguist

A specialist in the psychology of language and language development is called a psycholinguist.

Steven Pinker

Steven Pinker is most famous for his work on how children acquire language and for his modernization and popularization of Noam Chomsky's work on language as an innate faculty of mind. Pinker has suggested an evolutionary mental module for language, although this idea

remains controversial.

Instinct	Instinct is the word used to describe inherent dispositions towards particular actions. They are generally an inherited pattern of responses or reactions to certain kinds of situations.
Brain	The brain controls and coordinates most movement, behavior and homeostatic body functions such as heartbeat, blood pressure, fluid balance and body temperature. Functions of the brain are responsible for cognition, emotion, memory, motor learning and other sorts of learning. The brain is primarily made up of two types of cells: glia and neurons.
Variability	Statistically, variability refers to how much the scores in a distribution spread out, away from the mean.
Surface structure	In linguistics and syntax, surface structure refers to the representation derived from deep structure of a linguistic expression by transformational rules.
Deep structure	In linguistics, and especially the study of syntax, the deep structure of a linguistic expression is a theoretical construct that seeks to unify several related observed forms. In early transformational syntax, deep structures are derivation trees of a context free language. These trees are then transformed by a sequence of tree rewriting operations ("transformations") into surface structures.
Language acquisition device	The Language Acquisition Device is a part of the human brain theorized by Noam Chomsky which allows humans to acquire languages. This is a component of the nativist theory which suggests humans are born with the instinct or innate ability to acquire language.
Innate	Innate behavior is not learned or influenced by the environment, rather, it is present or predisposed at birth.
Constructivism	The view that individuals actively construct knowledge and understanding is referred to as constructivism.
Construct	A generalized concept, such as anxiety or gravity, is a construct.
Piaget	Piaget argued that young children's answers were qualitatively different than older children rather than quantitative. There are two major aspects to his theory: the process of coming to know and the stages we move through as we gradually acquire this ability.
Cognitive development	The process by which a child's understanding of the world changes as a function of age and experience is called cognitive development.
Cognition	The intellectual processes through which information is obtained, transformed, stored, retrieved, and otherwise used is cognition.
Gene	A gene is an ultramicroscopic area of the chromosome. It is the smallest physical unit of the DNA molecule that carries a piece of hereditary information.
Correlation	A statistical technique for determining the degree of association between two or more variables is referred to as correlation.
Perception	Perception is the process of acquiring, interpreting, selecting, and organizing sensory information.
Vygotsky	The Vygotsky model of human development has been termed as a sociocultural approach. The individual's development is a result of his or her culture.
Bruner	Bruner has had an enormous impact on educational psychology with his contributions to cognitive learning theory. His ideas are based on categorization, maintaining that people interpret the world in terms of its similarities and differences.
Language acquisition	The language acquisition support system is a conceptual system proposed by Bruner that suggests adults and older children have learning devices that interact with younger

Go to **Cram101.com** for the Practice Tests for this Chapter.

support system	children's language acquisition devices.
Hypothesis	A specific statement about behavior or mental processes that is testable through research is a hypothesis.
Stroke	A stroke occurs when the blood supply to a part of the brain is suddenly interrupted by occlusion, by hemorrhage, or other causes
Frontal lobe	The frontal lobe comprises four major folds of cortical tissue: the precentral gyrus, superior gyrus and the middle gyrus of the frontal gyri, the inferior frontal gyrus. It has been found to play a part in impulse control, judgement, language, memory, motor function, problem solving, sexual behavior, socialization and spontaneity.
Aphasia	Aphasia is a loss or impairment of the ability to produce or comprehend language, due to brain damage. It is usually a result of damage to the language centers of the brain.
Carl Wernicke	Carl Wernicke discovered the left cerebral hemisphere's speech centre.
Left hemisphere	The left hemisphere of the cortex controls the right side of the body, coordinates complex movements, and, in 95% of people, controls the production of speech and written language.
Right hemisphere	The brain is divided into left and right cerebral hemispheres. The right hemisphere of the cortex controls the left side of the body.
Cerebral cortex	The cerebral cortex is the outermost layer of the cerebrum and has a grey color. It is made up of four lobes and it is involved in many complex brain functions including memory, perceptual awareness, "thinking", language and consciousness. The cerebral cortex receives sensory information from many different sensory organs eg: eyes, ears, etc. and processes the information.
Severe mental retardation	A limitation in mental development as measured on the Wechsler Adult Intelligence Scale with scores between 20 -34 is called severe mental retardation.
Down syndrome	Down syndrome encompasses a number of genetic disorders, of which trisomy 21 (a nondisjunction, the so-called extrachromosone) is the most representative, causing highly variable degrees of learning difficulties as well as physical disabilities. Incidence of Down syndrome is estimated at 1 per 660 births, making it the most common chromosomal abnormality.
Syndrome	The term syndrome is the association of several clinically recognizable features, signs, symptoms, phenomena or characteristics which often occur together, so that the presence of one feature indicates the presence of the others.
Mental retardation	Mental retardation refers to having significantly below-average intellectual functioning and limitations in at least two areas of adaptive functioning. Many categorize retardation as mild, moderate, severe, or profound.
Pidgin	A Pidgin, or contact language, is the name given to any language created, usually spontaneously, out of a mixture of other languages as a means of communication between speakers of different tongues. Pidgins have simple grammars and few synonyms, serving as auxiliary contact languages. They are learned as second languages rather than natively.
American Sign Language	The American Sign Language is a language of hand gestures used by deaf and hearing impaired persons.
Fast mapping	In cognitive psychology, fast mapping is a mental process whereby a new concept can be learned based only on a single exposure to a given unit of information. Fast mapping is particularly important during language acquisition in young children, and serves (at least in part) to explain the prodigious rate at which children gain vocabulary.
Constructive processes	Constructive processes are processes in which memories are influenced by the meaning we give to events.

Go to **Cram101.com** for the Practice Tests for this Chapter.

Reinforcement	In operant conditioning, reinforcement is any change in an environment that (a) occurs after the behavior, (b) seems to make that behavior re-occur more often in the future and (c) that reoccurence of behavior must be the result of the change.
Inference	Inference is the act or process of drawing a conclusion based solely on what one already knows.

Go to **Cram101.com** for the Practice Tests for this Chapter.

Marcia	Marcia argued that identity could be viewed as a structure of beliefs, abilities and past experiences regarding the self. Identity is a dynamic, not static structure. At least three aspects of the adolescent's development are important in identity formation: must be confident that they have parental support, must have an established sense of industry, and must be able to adopt a self-reflective stance toward the future.
Early childhood	Early childhood refers to the developmental period extending from the end of infancy to about 5 or 6 years of age; sometimes called the preschool years.
Maturation	The orderly unfolding of traits, as regulated by the genetic code is called maturation.
Variability	Statistically, variability refers to how much the scores in a distribution spread out, away from the mean.
Society	The social sciences use the term society to mean a group of people that form a semi-closed (or semi-open) social system, in which most interactions are with other individuals belonging to the group.
Puberty	Puberty refers to the process of physical changes by which a child's body becomes an adult body capable of reproduction.
Toddler	A toddler is a child between the ages of one and three years old. During this period, the child learns a great deal about social roles and develops motor skills; to toddle is to walk unsteadily.
Brain	The brain controls and coordinates most movement, behavior and homeostatic body functions such as heartbeat, blood pressure, fluid balance and body temperature. Functions of the brain are responsible for cognition, emotion, memory, motor learning and other sorts of learning. The brain is primarily made up of two types of cells: glia and neurons.
Problem solving	An attempt to find an appropriate way of attaining a goal when the goal is not readily available is called problem solving.
Neural impulse	Neural impulse refers to the electrochemical discharge of a nerve cell, or neuron.
Myelination	The process in which the nerve cells are covered and insulated with a layer of fat cells, which increases the speed at which information travels through the nervous system is referred to as myelination.
Association areas	Association areas refer to the site of the higher mental processes such as thought, language, memory, and speech.
Nervous system	The body's electrochemical communication circuitry, made up of billions of neurons is a nervous system.
Dendrite	A dendrite is a slender, typically branched projection of a nerve cell, or "neuron," which conducts the electrical stimulation received from other cells to the body or soma of the cell from which it projects. This stimulation arrives through synapses, which typically are located near the tips of the dendrites and away from the soma.
Cognitive development	The process by which a child's understanding of the world changes as a function of age and experience is called cognitive development.
Piaget	Piaget argued that young children's answers were qualitatively different than older children rather than quantitative. There are two major aspects to his theory: the process of coming to know and the stages we move through as we gradually acquire this ability.
Egocentrism	The inability to distinguish between one's own perspective and someone else's is referred to as egocentrism.
Adolescence	The period of life bounded by puberty and the assumption of adult responsibilities is

adolescence.

Reasoning	Reasoning is the act of using reason to derive a conclusion from certain premises. There are two main methods to reach a conclusion,deductive reasoning and inductive reasoning.
Moral reasoning	Moral reasoning involves concepts of justice, whereas social conventional judgments are concepts of social organization.
Preoperational stage	The Preoperational stage is the second stage of development in Piaget's theory. By observing sequences of play, Piaget was able to demonstrate that towards the end of the second year a qualitatively quite new kind of functioning occurs. Operation in Piagetian theory is any procedure for mentally acting on objects.
Infancy	The developmental period that extends from birth to 18 or 24 months is called infancy.
Attention	Attention is the cognitive process of selectively concentrating on one thing while ignoring other things. Psychologists have labeled three types of attention: sustained attention, selective attention, and divided attention.
Concrete operational	According to Piaget, the period from 7 to 12 years of age, which is characterized by logical thought and a loss of egocentrism, is referred to as concrete operational stage. Conservation skills are formed - understanding that quantity, length or number of items is unrelated to the appearance of the object or items.
Transductive reasoning	Reasoning from the specific to the specific is called transductive reasoning. It is typically employed by children.
Inductive reasoning	A form of reasoning in which we reason from individual cases or particular facts to a general conclusion is referred to as inductive reasoning. The conclusion can be said to follow with a probability rather than certainty.
Reliability	Reliability means the extent to which a test produces a consistent , reproducible score .
Script	A schema, or behavioral sequence, for an event is called a script. It is a form of schematic organization, with real-world events organized in terms of temporal and causal relations between component acts.
Punishment	Punishment is the addtion of a stimulus that reduces the frequency of a response, or the removal of a stimulus that results in a reduction of the response.
Analogy	An analogy is a comparison between two different things, in order to highlight some form of similarity. Analogy is the cognitive process of transferring information from a particular subject to another particular subject.
Theories	Theories are logically self-consistent models or frameworks describing the behavior of a certain natural or social phenomenon. They are broad explanations and predictions concerning phenomena of interest.
Acquisition	Acquisition is the process of adapting to the environment, learning or becoming conditioned. In classical conditoning terms, it is the initial learning of the stimulus response link, which involves a neutral stimulus being associated with a unconditioned stimulus and becoming a conditioned stimulus.
Learning	Learning is a relatively permanent change in behavior that results from experience. Thus, to attribute a behavioral change to learning, the change must be relatively permanent and must result from experience.
Sensory register	Sensory register involves two components: iconic memory: the storage of visual information, lasting about half a second; and, echoic memory: the storage of auditory information, lasting up to two seconds. Information from the environment is filtered through this sensory register and passed on to the short-term memory circuit.

Retrieval	Retrieval is the location of stored information and its subsequent return to consciousness. It is the third stage of information processing.
Working Memory	Working memory is the collection of structures and processes in the brain used for temporarily storing and manipulating information. Working memory consists of both memory for items that are currently being processed, and components governing attention and directing the processing itself.
Long term memory	Long term memory is memory that lasts from over 30 seconds to years.
Information processing	Information processing is an approach to the goal of understanding human thinking. The essence of the approach is to see cognition as being essentially computational in nature, with mind being the software and the brain being the hardware.
Affect	A subjective feeling or emotional tone often accompanied by bodily expressions noticeable to others is called affect.
Knowledge base	The general background information a person possesses, which influences most cognitive task performance is called the knowledge base.
Stages	Stages represent relatively discrete periods of time in which functioning is qualitatively different from functioning at other periods.
Species	Species refers to a reproductively isolated breeding population.
Habituation	In habituation there is a progressive reduction in the response probability with continued repetition of a stimulus.
Sullivan	Sullivan developed the Self System, a configuration of the personality traits developed in childhood and reinforced by positive affirmation and the security operations developed in childhood to avoid anxiety and threats to self-esteem.
Emotion	An emotion is a mental states that arise spontaneously, rather than through conscious effort. They are often accompanied by physiological changes.
Social referencing	Social referencing refers to the process by which infants use the nonverbal emotional expressions of a caregiver as cues to guide their behavior.
Pretend play	According to Piaget and Smilansky, pretend play is the third cognitive level of play. It involves imaginary people or situations.
Perception	Perception is the process of acquiring, interpreting, selecting, and organizing sensory information.
Chomsky	Chomsky has greatly influenced the field of theoretical linguistics with his work on the theory of generative grammar. Accordingly, humans are biologically prewired to learn language at a certain time and in a certain way.
Innate	Innate behavior is not learned or influenced by the environment, rather, it is present or predisposed at birth.
Gene	A gene is an ultramicroscopic area of the chromosome. It is the smallest physical unit of the DNA molecule that carries a piece of hereditary information.
Qualitative change	A qualitative change refers to a change in kind, structure, or organization, such as the change from nonverbal to verbal communication.
Autism	Autism is a neurodevelopmental disorder that manifests itself in markedly abnormal social interaction, communication ability, patterns of interests, and patterns of behavior.
Evolution	Commonly used to refer to gradual change, evolution is the change in the frequency of alleles within a population from one generation to the next. This change may be caused by different

mechanisms, including natural selection, genetic drift, or changes in population (gene flow).

Senses	The senses are systems that consist of a sensory cell type that respond to a specific kind of physical energy, and that correspond to a defined region within the brain where the signals are received and interpreted.
Schema	Schema refers to a way of mentally representing the world, such as a belief or an expectation, that can influence perception of persons, objects, and situations.
Social role	Social role refers to expected behavior patterns associated with particular social positions.
Construct	A generalized concept, such as anxiety or gravity, is a construct.
Theory of mind	A theory of mind considers the nature of mind, and its structure and processes
Standardized test	An oral or written assessment for which an individual receives a score indicating how the individual reponded relative to a previously tested large sample of others is referred to as a standardized test.
Mental processes	The thoughts, feelings, and motives that each of us experiences privately but that cannot be observed directly are called mental processes.
Population	Population refers to all members of a well-defined group of organisms, events, or things.
Survey	A method of scientific investigation in which a large sample of people answer questions about their attitudes or behavior is referred to as a survey.
Attitude	An enduring mental representation of a person, place, or thing that evokes an emotional response and related behavior is called attitude.
Magical thinking	Magical thinking is a term used to describe non-scientific causal reasoning. Magical thinking depends on two laws: the law of similarity (an effect resembles its cause), and the law of contagion (things which were once in physical contact maintain a connection even after physical contact has been broken).
Cognition	The intellectual processes through which information is obtained, transformed, stored, retrieved, and otherwise used is cognition.
Developmental psychologist	A psychologist interested in human growth and development from conception until death is referred to as a developmental psychologist.
Wave theory	Békésy's, in his wave theory, argued that different sound wave frequencies are locally dispersed before exciting different nerve fibers that lead from the cochlea to the brain. He theorized that the placement of each sensory cell (hair cell) along the coil of the cochlea corresponds to a specific frequency of sound.
Egocentric thought	A way of thinking in which the child views the world entirely from his or her own perspective is referred to as egocentric thought.
Hypothesis	A specific statement about behavior or mental processes that is testable through research is a hypothesis.
Shaping	The concept of reinforcing successive, increasingly accurate approximations to a target behavior is called shaping. The target behavior is broken down into a hierarchy of elemental steps, each step more sophisticated then the last. By successively reinforcing each of the the elemental steps, a form of differential reinforcement, until that step is learned while extinguishing the step below, the target behavior is gradually achieved.

Internalization	The developmental change from behavior that is externally controlled to behavior that is controlled by internal standards and principles is referred to as internalization.
Learning	Learning is a relatively permanent change in behavior that results from experience. Thus, to attribute a behavioral change to learning, the change must be relatively permanent and must result from experience.
Social development	The person's developing capacity for social relationships and the effects of those relationships on further development is referred to as social development.
Socialization	Social rules and social relations are created, communicated, and changed in verbal and nonverbal ways creating social complexity useful in identifying outsiders and intelligent breeding partners. The process of learning these skills is called socialization.
Society	The social sciences use the term society to mean a group of people that form a semi-closed (or semi-open) social system, in which most interactions are with other individuals belonging to the group.
Personality	Personality refers to the pattern of enduring characteristics that differentiates a person, the patterns of behaviors that make each individual unique.
Interdependence	Interdependence is a dynamic of being mutually responsible to and dependent on others.
Social role	Social role refers to expected behavior patterns associated with particular social positions.
Identical twins	Identical twins occur when a single egg is fertilized to form one zygote (monozygotic) but the zygote then divides into two separate embryos. The two embryos develop into foetuses sharing the same womb. Monozygotic twins are genetically identical unless there has been a mutation in development, and they are almost always the same gender.
Temperament	Temperament refers to a basic, innate disposition to change behavior. The activity level is an important dimension of temperament.
Trait	An enduring personality characteristic that tends to lead to certain behaviors is called a trait. The term trait also means a genetically inherited feature of an organism.
Habit	A habit is a response that has become completely separated from its eliciting stimulus. Early learning theorists used the term to describe S-R associations, however not all S-R associations become a habit, rather many are extinguished after reinforcement is withdrawn.
Norms	In testing, standards of test performance that permit the comparison of one person's score on the test to the scores of others who have taken the same test are referred to as norms.
Attention	Attention is the cognitive process of selectively concentrating on one thing while ignoring other things. Psychologists have labeled three types of attention: sustained attention, selective attention, and divided attention.
Early childhood	Early childhood refers to the developmental period extending from the end of infancy to about 5 or 6 years of age; sometimes called the preschool years.
Emotion	An emotion is a mental states that arise spontaneously, rather than through conscious effort. They are often accompanied by physiological changes.
Innate	Innate behavior is not learned or influenced by the environment, rather, it is present or predisposed at birth.
Personal identity	The portion of the self-concept that pertains to the self as a distinct, separate individual is called personal identity.
Clique	A clique is an informal and restricted social group formed by a number of people who share common. Social roles vary, but two roles commonly associated with a female clique is notably applicable to most - that of the "queen bee" and that of the "outcast".

Acquisition	Acquisition is the process of adapting to the environment, learning or becoming conditioned. In classical conditoning terms, it is the initial learning of the stimulus response link, which involves a neutral stimulus being associated with a unconditioned stimulus and becoming a conditioned stimulus.
Developmental psychologist	A psychologist interested in human growth and development from conception until death is referred to as a developmental psychologist.
Psychodynamic	Most psychodynamic approaches are centered around the idea of a maladapted function developed early in life (usually childhood) which are at least in part unconscious. This maladapted function (a.k.a. defense mechanism) does not do well in place of a normal/healthy one.
Infancy	The developmental period that extends from birth to 18 or 24 months is called infancy.
Phallic stage	The phallic stage is the 3rd of Freud's psychosexual stages, when awareness of and manipulation of the genitals is supposed to be a primary source of pleasure. In this stage the child deals with the Oedipus complex, if male, or the Electra Complex, if female.
Anal stage	The anal stage in psychology is the term used by Sigmund Freud to describe the development during the second year of life, in which a child's pleasure and conflict centers are in the anal area.
Stages	Stages represent relatively discrete periods of time in which functioning is qualitatively different from functioning at other periods.
Genitals	Genitals refers to the internal and external reproductive organs.
Masculinity	Masculinity is a culturally determined value reflecting the set of characteristics of maleness.
Oedipus complex	The Oedipus complex is a concept developed by Sigmund Freud to explain the maturation of the infant boy through identification with the father and desire for the mother.
Guilt	Guilt describes many concepts related to a negative emotion or condition caused by actions which are believed to be, morally wrong. According to Freud, the avoidance of guilt is the basis for moral behavior.
Penis	The penis is the external male copulatory organ and the external male organ of urination. In humans, the penis is homologous to the female clitoris, as it develops from the same embryonic structure. It is capable of erection for use in copulation.
Trauma	Trauma refers to a severe physical injury or wound to the body caused by an external force, or a psychological shock having a lasting effect on mental life.
Psychological trauma	Psychological trauma involves a singular experience or enduring event or events that completely overwhelm the individual's ability to cope or integrate the emotion involved with that experience. It usually involves a complete feeling of helplessness in the face of a real or subjective threat to life, bodily integrity, or sanity.
Theories	Theories are logically self-consistent models or frameworks describing the behavior of a certain natural or social phenomenon. They are broad explanations and predictions concerning phenomena of interest.
Longitudinal study	Longitudinal study is a type of developmental study in which the same group of participants is followed and measured for an extended period of time, often years.
Modeling	A type of behavior learned through observation of others demonstrating the same behavior is modeling.
Differential reinforcement	Any training procedure in which certain kinds of behavior are systematically reinforced and others are not is called differential reinforcement. Differential reinforcement involves both

	reinforcement and extinction.
Reinforcement	In operant conditioning, reinforcement is any change in an environment that (a) occurs after the behavior, (b) seems to make that behavior re-occur more often in the future and (c) that reoccurence of behavior must be the result of the change.
Stereotype	A stereotype is considered to be a group concept, held by one social group about another.They are often used in a negative or prejudicial sense and are frequently used to justify certain discriminatory behaviors. This allows powerful social groups to legitimize and protect their dominant position
Gender stereotypes	Broad categories that reflect our impressions and beliefs about typical females and males are referred to as gender stereotypes.
Kohlberg	Kohlberg believed that people progressed in their moral reasoning through a series of developmental stages.
Piaget	Piaget argued that young children's answers were qualitatively different than older children rather than quantitative. There are two major aspects to his theory: the process of coming to know and the stages we move through as we gradually acquire this ability.
Cognitive development	The process by which a child's understanding of the world changes as a function of age and experience is called cognitive development.
Gender schema	Gender schema refers to a cognitive structure that organizes the world in terms of maleness and femaleness.
Schema Theory	According to Schema Theory, people mold memories to fit information that already exists in their minds. This process is guided by schemes, which are mental frameworks that serve to organize concepts and information.
Schema	Schema refers to a way of mentally representing the world, such as a belief or an expectation, that can influence perception of persons, objects, and situations.
Gender schema theory	The theory that an individual's attention and behavior are guided by an internal motivation to conform to gender-based sociocultural standards and stereotypes is the Gender Schema Theory.
Affect	A subjective feeling or emotional tone often accompanied by bodily expressions noticeable to others is called affect.
Cognitive structure	According to Piaget, the number of schemata available to an organism at any given time constitutes that organism's cognitive structure. How the organism interacts with its environment depends on the current cognitive structure available. As the cognitive structure develops, new assimilations can occur.
Script	A schema, or behavioral sequence, for an event is called a script. It is a form of schematic organization, with real-world events organized in terms of temporal and causal relations between component acts.
Shaping	The concept of reinforcing successive, increasingly accurate approximations to a target behavior is called shaping. The target behavior is broken down into a hierarchy of elemental steps, each step more sophisticated then the last. By successively reinforcing each of the the elemental steps, a form of differential reinforcement, until that step is learned while extinguishing the step below, the target behavior is gradually achieved.
Ethnic identity	An enduring, basic aspect of the self that includes a sense of membership in an ethnic group and the attitudes and feelings related to that membership is called an ethnic identity.
Ethnic group	An ethnic group is a culture or subculture whose members are readily distinguishable by outsiders based on traits originating from a common racial, national, linguistic, or

religious source. Members of an ethnic group are often presumed to be culturally or biologically similar, although this is not in fact necessarily the case.

Attitude	An enduring mental representation of a person, place, or thing that evokes an emotional response and related behavior is called attitude.
Ethnicity	Ethnicity refers to a characteristic based on cultural heritage, nationality characteristics, race, religion, and language.
Bias	A bias is a prejudice in a general or specific sense, usually in the sense for having a preference to one particular point of view or ideological perspective.
Reflection	Reflection is the process of rephrasing or repeating thoughts and feelings expressed, making the person more aware of what they are saying or thinking.
Discrimination	In Learning theory, discrimination refers the ability to distinguish between a conditioned stimulus and other stimuli. It can be brought about by extensive training or differential reinforcement. In social terms, it is the denial of privileges to a person or a group on the basis of prejudice.
Prejudice	Prejudice in general, implies coming to a judgment on the subject before learning where the preponderance of the evidence actually lies, or formation of a judgement without direct experience.
Questionnaire	A self-report method of data collection or clinical assessment method in which the individual being studied checks off items on a printed list, answers multiple-choice questions, or writes out answers to essay questions aimed at producing a selfdescription is called questionnaire.
Adolescence	The period of life bounded by puberty and the assumption of adult responsibilities is adolescence.
Autobiograph-cal memory	An Autobiographical Memory is a personal representation of general or specific events and personal facts.
Domain Theory	Within domain theory a distinction is drawn between the child's developing concepts of morality, and other domains of social knowledge, such as social convention. According to domain theory, the child's concepts of morality and social convention emerge out of the child's attempts to account for qualitatively differing forms of social experience associated with these two classes of social events.
Heteronomous	From his observations, Piaget concluded that children begin in a heteronomous stage of moral reasoning, characterized by a strict adherence to rules and duties, and obedience to authority.
Conformity	Conformity is the degree to which members of a group will change their behavior, views and attitudes to fit the views of the group. The group can influence members via unconscious processes or via overt social pressure on individuals.
Autonomous morality	According to Piaget's theory of moral development, during the second stage the child enters autonomous morality. The child becomes aware that rules and laws are created by people and that, in judging an action, one should consider the actor's intentions as well as the consequence.
Moral development	Development regarding rules and conventions about what people should do in their interactions with other people is called moral development.
Normative	The term normative is used to describe the effects of those structures of culture which regulate the function of social activity.
Sigmund Freud	Sigmund Freud was the founder of the psychoanalytic school, based on his theory that

	unconscious motives control much behavior, that particular kinds of unconscious thoughts and memories are the source of neurosis, and that neurosis could be treated through bringing these unconscious thoughts and memories to consciousness in psychoanalytic treatment.
Ego	In Freud's view the Ego serves to balance our primitive needs and our moral beliefs and taboos. Relying on experience, a healthy Ego provides the ability to adapt to reality and interact with the outside world.
Superego	Frued's third psychic structure, which functions as a moral guardian and sets forth high standards for behavior is the superego.
Punishment	Punishment is the addtion of a stimulus that reduces the frequency of a response, or the removal of a stimulus that results in a reduction of the response.
Problem solving	An attempt to find an appropriate way of attaining a goal when the goal is not readily available is called problem solving.
Logical thought	Drawing conclusions on the basis of formal principles of reasoning is referred to as logical thought.
Perception	Perception is the process of acquiring, interpreting, selecting, and organizing sensory information.
Adaptation	Adaptation is a lowering of sensitivity to a stimulus following prolonged exposure to that stimulus. Behavioral adaptations are special ways a particular organism behaves to survive in its natural habitat.
Friendship	The essentials of friendship are reciprocity and commitment between individuals who see themselves more or less as equals. Interaction between friends rests on a more equal power base than the interaction between children and adults.
Attention deficit hyperactivity disorder	A learning disability marked by inattention, impulsiveness, a low tolerance for frustration, and a great deal of inappropriate activity is the attention deficit hyperactivity disorder.
Hyperactivity	Hyperactivity can be described as a state in which a individual is abnormally easily excitable and exuberant. Strong emotional reactions and a very short span of attention is also typical for the individual.
Individual differences	Individual differences psychology studies the ways in which individual people differ in their behavior. This is distinguished from other aspects of psychology in that although psychology is ostensibly a study of individuals, modern psychologists invariably study groups.
Situational compliance	Obedience of a parent's orders only in the presence of prompting or other signs of ongoing parental control is situational compliance.
Vygotsky	The Vygotsky model of human development has been termed as a sociocultural approach. The individual's development is a result of his or her culture.
Zone of proximal development	The zone of proximal development is the gap between a learner's current or actual level of development determined by independent problem solving and the learner's emerging or potential level of development. Learners cannot build new knowledge without first having a framework or prior learning foundation.
Proximal	Students can set both long-term (distal) and short-term (proximal) goals .
Evolution	Commonly used to refer to gradual change, evolution is the change in the frequency of alleles within a population from one generation to the next. This change may be caused by different mechanisms, including natural selection, genetic drift, or changes in population (gene flow).

131

Species	Species refers to a reproductively isolated breeding population.
Lorenz	Lorenz demonstrated how incubator-hatched geese would imprint on the first suitable moving stimulus they saw within what he called a "critical period" of about 36 hours shortly after hatching. Most famously, the goslings would imprint on Lorenz himself .
Darwin	Darwin achieved lasting fame as originator of the theory of evolution through natural selection. His book Expression of Emotions in Man and Animals is generally considered the first text on comparative psychology.
Gene	A gene is an ultramicroscopic area of the chromosome. It is the smallest physical unit of the DNA molecule that carries a piece of hereditary information.
Testosterone	Testosterone is a steroid hormone from the androgen group. It is the principal male sex hormone and the "original" anabolic steroid.
Hormone	A hormone is a chemical messenger from one cell (or group of cells) to another. The best known are those produced by endocrine glands, but they are produced by nearly every organ system. The function of hormones is to serve as a signal to the target cells; the action of the hormone is determined by the pattern of secretion and the signal transduction of the receiving tissue.
Correlation	A statistical technique for determining the degree of association between two or more variables is referred to as correlation.
Brain	The brain controls and coordinates most movement, behavior and homeostatic body functions such as heartbeat, blood pressure, fluid balance and body temperature. Functions of the brain are responsible for cognition, emotion, memory, motor learning and other sorts of learning. The brain is primarily made up of two types of cells: glia and neurons.
Reasoning	Reasoning is the act of using reason to derive a conclusion from certain premises. There are two main methods to reach a conclusion, deductive reasoning and inductive reasoning.
Anxiety	Anxiety is a complex combination of the feeling of fear, apprehension and worry often accompanied by physical sensations such as palpitations, chest pain and/or shortness of breath.
Observational learning	The acquisition of knowledge and skills through the observation of others rather than by means of direct experience is observational learning. Four major processes are thought to influence the observational learning: attentional, retentional, behavioral production, and motivational.
Prototype	A concept of a category of objects or events that serves as a good example of the category is called a prototype.
Naturalistic observation	Naturalistic observation is a method of observation that involves observing subjects in their natural habitats. Researchers take great care in avoiding making interferences with the behavior they are observing by using unobtrusive methods.
Hypothesis	A specific statement about behavior or mental processes that is testable through research is a hypothesis.
Catharsis	Catharsis has been adopted by modern psychotherapy as the act of giving expression to deep emotions often associated with events in the individuals past which have never before been adequately expressed.
Empathy	Empathy is the recognition and understanding of the states of mind, including beliefs, desires and particularly emotions of others without injecting your own.
Sympathetic	The sympathetic nervous system activates what is often termed the "fight or flight response". It is an automatic regulation system, that is, one that operates without the intervention of

	conscious thought.
Social skills	Social skills are skills used to interact and communicate with others to assist status in the social structure and other motivations.
Emotional regulation	Techniques for controlling one's emotional states to efficiently adapt and reach a goal is called emotional regulation.
Variable	A variable refers to a measurable factor, characteristic, or attribute of an individual or a system.
Arousal	Arousal is a physiological and psychological state involving the activation of the reticular activating system in the brain stem, the autonomic nervous system and the endocrine system, leading to increased heart rate and blood pressure and a condition of alertness and readiness to respond.
Social influence	Social influence is when the actions or thoughts of individual(s) are changed by other individual(s). Peer pressure is an example of social influence.
Attachment	Attachment is the tendency to seek closeness to another person and feel secure when that person is present.
Evolutionary perspective	A perspective that focuses on how humans have evolved and adapted behaviors required for survival against various environmental pressures over the long course is called the evolutionary perspective.

Gene	A gene is an ultramicroscopic area of the chromosome. It is the smallest physical unit of the DNA molecule that carries a piece of hereditary information.
Malnutrition	Malnutrition is a general term for the medical condition in a person or animal caused by an unbalanced diet—either too little or too much food, or a diet missing one or more important nutrients.
UNICEF	UNICEF, the United Nations International Children's Emergency Fund, was established by the United Nations General Assembly on December 11, 1946. UNICEF provides long-term humanitarian and developmental assistance to children and mothers in developing countries.
Acute	Acute means sudden, sharp, and abrupt. Usually short in duration.
Early childhood	Early childhood refers to the developmental period extending from the end of infancy to about 5 or 6 years of age; sometimes called the preschool years.
Toddler	A toddler is a child between the ages of one and three years old. During this period, the child learns a great deal about social roles and develops motor skills; to toddle is to walk unsteadily.
Microsystem	The setting or context in which an individual lives, including the person's family, peers, school, and neighborhood is a microsystem.
Society	The social sciences use the term society to mean a group of people that form a semi-closed (or semi-open) social system, in which most interactions are with other individuals belonging to the group.
Temperament	Temperament refers to a basic, innate disposition to change behavior. The activity level is an important dimension of temperament.
Shaping	The concept of reinforcing successive, increasingly accurate approximations to a target behavior is called shaping. The target behavior is broken down into a hierarchy of elemental steps, each step more sophisticated then the last. By successively reinforcing each of the the elemental steps, a form of differential reinforcement, until that step is learned while extinguishing the step below, the target behavior is gradually achieved.
Social development	The person's developing capacity for social relationships and the effects of those relationships on further development is referred to as social development.
Polygyny	Polygyny is a marital practice in which a man has more than one wife simultaneously.
Attention	Attention is the cognitive process of selectively concentrating on one thing while ignoring other things. Psychologists have labeled three types of attention: sustained attention, selective attention, and divided attention.
Attachment	Attachment is the tendency to seek closeness to another person and feel secure when that person is present.
Lesbian	A lesbian is a homosexual woman. They are women who are sexually and romantically attracted to other women.
Affect	A subjective feeling or emotional tone often accompanied by bodily expressions noticeable to others is called affect.
Social role	Social role refers to expected behavior patterns associated with particular social positions.
Social support	Social Support is the physical and emotional comfort given by family, friends, co-workers and others. Research has identified three main types of social support: emotional, practical, sharing points of view.
Population	Population refers to all members of a well-defined group of organisms, events, or things.

Go to **Cram101.com** for the Practice Tests for this Chapter.

Socioeconomic	Socioeconomic pertains to the study of the social and economic impacts of any product or service offering, market intervention or other activity on an economy as a whole and on the companies, organization and individuals who are its main economic actors.
Ethnicity	Ethnicity refers to a characteristic based on cultural heritage, nationality characteristics, race, religion, and language.
Social skills	Social skills are skills used to interact and communicate with others to assist status in the social structure and other motivations.
Cultural values	The importance and desirability of various objects and activities as defined by people in a given culture are referred to as cultural values.
Ecology	Ecology refers to the branch of biology that deals with the relationships between living organisms and their environment.
Infant mortality	Infant mortality is the death of infants in the first year of life. The leading causes of infant mortality are dehydration and disease. Major causes of infant mortality in more developed countries include congenital malformation, infection and SIDS. Infant mortality rate is the number of newborns dying under a year of age divided by the number of live births during the year.
Authoritative parenting	Authoritative parenting encourages children to be independent but still places limits and controls on their actions. Extensive verbal give-and-take is allowed, and parents are warm and nurturant toward the child.
Authoritarian	The term authoritarian is used to describe a style that enforces strong and sometimes oppressive measures against those in its sphere of influence, generally without attempts at gaining their consent.
Punishment	Punishment is the addtion of a stimulus that reduces the frequency of a response, or the removal of a stimulus that results in a reduction of the response.
Obedience	Obedience is the willingness to follow the will of others. Humans have been shown to be surprisingly obedient in the presence of perceived legitimate authority figures, as demonstrated by the Milgram experiment in the 1960s.
Authoritative parents	Authoritative parents are strict and warm. Authoritative parents demand mature behavior but use reason rather than force in discipline.
Authoritarian parents	Parents who are rigid in their rules and who demand obedience for the sake of obedience are called authoritarian parents.
Permissive parents	Parents who impose few, if any, rules and who do not supervise their children closely are called permissive parents.
Impulse control	Deferred gratification is the ability of a person to wait for things they want. This trait is critical for life success. Those who lack this trait are said to suffer from poor impulse control, and often become criminals, as they are unwilling to work and wait for their paycheck.
Authoritarian parenting	Authoritarian parenting is a restrictive punitive style in which parents urge the child to follow their directions and to respect work and effort. Authoritarian parenting places firm limits and controls on the child and allows little verbal exchange.
Socialization	Social rules and social relations are created, communicated, and changed in verbal and nonverbal ways creating social complexity useful in identifying outsiders and intelligent breeding partners. The process of learning these skills is called socialization.
Social ecology	The entire network of interactions and interdependencies among people, institutions, and cultural constructs to which the developing person must adapt psychologically is called the

social ecology.

Subjective experience	Subjective experience refers to reality as it is perceived and interpreted, not as it exists objectively.
Hypothesis	A specific statement about behavior or mental processes that is testable through research is a hypothesis.
Positive relationship	Statistically, a positive relationship refers to a mathematical relationship in which increases in one measure are matched by increases in the other.
Questionnaire	A self-report method of data collection or clinical assessment method in which the individual being studied checks off items on a printed list, answers multiple-choice questions, or writes out answers to essay questions aimed at producing a selfdescription is called questionnaire.
Socioeconomic Status	A family's socioeconomic status is based on family income, parental education level, parental occupation, and social status in the community. Those with high status often have more success in preparing their children for school because they have access to a wide range of resources.
Case study	A carefully drawn biography that may be obtained through interviews, questionnaires, and psychological tests is called a case study.
Ideology	An ideology can be thought of as a comprehensive vision, as a way of looking at things, as in common sense and several philosophical tendencies, or a set of ideas proposed by the dominant class of a society to all members of this society.
Discrimination	In Learning theory, discrimination refers the ability to distinguish between a conditioned stimulus and other stimuli. It can be brought about by extensive training or differential reinforcement. In social terms, it is the denial of privileges to a person or a group on the basis of prejudice.
Sexual orientation	Sexual orientation refers to the sex or gender of people who are the focus of a person's amorous or erotic desires, fantasies, and spontaneous feelings, the gender(s) toward which one is primarily "oriented".
Gender identity	Gender identity describes the gender with which a person identifies, but can also be used to refer to the gender that other people attribute to the individual on the basis of what they know from gender role indications.
Moral reasoning	Moral reasoning involves concepts of justice, whereas social conventional judgments are concepts of social organization.
Personality	Personality refers to the pattern of enduring characteristics that differentiates a person, the patterns of behaviors that make each individual unique.
Reasoning	Reasoning is the act of using reason to derive a conclusion from certain premises. There are two main methods to reach a conclusion,deductive reasoning and inductive reasoning.
Locus of control	The place to which an individual attributes control over the receiving of reinforcers -either inside or outside the self is referred to as locus of control.
Stages	Stages represent relatively discrete periods of time in which functioning is qualitatively different from functioning at other periods.
Cognitive skills	Cognitive skills such as reasoning, attention, and memory can be advanced and sustained through practice and training.
Depression	In everyday language depression refers to any downturn in mood, which may be relatively transitory and perhaps due to something trivial. This is differentiated from Clinical

	depression which is marked by symptoms that last two weeks or more and are so severe that they interfere with daily living.
Major depression	Major depression is characterized by a severely depressed mood that persists for at least two weeks. Episodes of depression may start suddenly or slowly and can occur several times through a person's life. The disorder may be categorized as "single episode" or "recurrent" depending on whether previous episodes have been experienced before.
Asthma	Asthma is a complex disease characterized by bronchial hyperresponsiveness (BHR), inflammation, mucus production and intermittent airway obstruction.
Standardized test	An oral or written assessment for which an individual receives a score indicating how the individual reponded relative to a previously tested large sample of others is referred to as a standardized test.
Protective factors	Protective factors are influences that reduce the impact of early stress and tend to lead to positive outcomes.
Trauma	Trauma refers to a severe physical injury or wound to the body caused by an external force, or a psychological shock having a lasting effect on mental life.
Individual differences	Individual differences psychology studies the ways in which individual people differ in their behavior. This is distinguished from other aspects of psychology in that although psychology is ostensibly a study of individuals, modern psychologists invariably study groups.
Child abuse	Child abuse is the physical or psychological maltreatment of a child.
Child maltreatment	Actions that harm children either physically or psychologically are referred to as child maltreatment and include: physical abuse, sexual abuse, child neglect, and emotional abuse.
Sexual abuse	Sexual abuse is a term used to describe non- consentual sexual relations between two or more parties which are considered criminally and/or morally offensive.
Emotion	An emotion is a mental states that arise spontaneously, rather than through conscious effort. They are often accompanied by physiological changes.
Neglected children	Neglected children are infrequently nominated as a best friend but are not disliked by their peers.
Nightmare	Nightmare was the original term for the state later known as waking dream, and more currently as sleep paralysis, associated with rapid eye movement (REM) periods of sleep.
Bias	A bias is a prejudice in a general or specific sense, usually in the sense for having a preference to one particular point of view or ideological perspective.
Control group	A group that does not receive the treatment effect in an experiment is referred to as the control group or sometimes as the comparison group.
Personal identity	The portion of the self-concept that pertains to the self as a distinct, separate individual is called personal identity.
Acquisition	Acquisition is the process of adapting to the environment, learning or becoming conditioned. In classical conditoning terms, it is the initial learning of the stimulus response link, which involves a neutral stimulus being associated with a unconditioned stimulus and becoming a conditioned stimulus.
Autonomy	Autonomy is the condition of something that does not depend on anything else.
Naturalistic observation	Naturalistic observation is a method of observation that involves observing subjects in their natural habitats. Researchers take great care in avoiding making interferences with the behavior they are observing by using unobtrusive methods.

Sensation	Sensation is the first stage in the chain of biochemical and neurologic events that begins with the impinging of a stimulus upon the receptor cells of a sensory organ, which then leads to perception, the mental state that is reflected in statements like "I see a uniformly blue wall."
Roger Barker	In his classic work "Ecological Psychology" (1968), Roger Barker argued that human behavior was radically situated: in other words, you couldn't make predictions about human behavior unless you know what situation or context or environment the human in question was in.
Attention	Attention is the cognitive process of selectively concentrating on one thing while ignoring other things. Psychologists have labeled three types of attention: sustained attention, selective attention, and divided attention.
Child development	Scientific study of the processes of change from conception through adolescence is called child development.
Society	The social sciences use the term society to mean a group of people that form a semi-closed (or semi-open) social system, in which most interactions are with other individuals belonging to the group.
Acquisition	Acquisition is the process of adapting to the environment, learning or becoming conditioned. In classical conditoning terms, it is the initial learning of the stimulus response link, which involves a neutral stimulus being associated with a unconditioned stimulus and becoming a conditioned stimulus.
Social norm	A social norm, is a rule that is socially enforced. In social situations, such as meetings, they are unwritten and often unstated rules that govern individuals' behavior. A social norm is most evident when not followed or broken.
Norms	In testing, standards of test performance that permit the comparison of one person's score on the test to the scores of others who have taken the same test are referred to as norms.
Cognitive skills	Cognitive skills such as reasoning, attention, and memory can be advanced and sustained through practice and training.
Brain	The brain controls and coordinates most movement, behavior and homeostatic body functions such as heartbeat, blood pressure, fluid balance and body temperature. Functions of the brain are responsible for cognition, emotion, memory, motor learning and other sorts of learning. The brain is primarily made up of two types of cells: glia and neurons.
Theories	Theories are logically self-consistent models or frameworks describing the behavior of a certain natural or social phenomenon. They are broad explanations and predictions concerning phenomena of interest.
Adolescence	The period of life bounded by puberty and the assumption of adult responsibilities is adolescence.
Monozygotic	Identical twins occur when a single egg is fertilized to form one zygote, calld monozygotic, but the zygote then divides into two separate embryos. The two embryos develop into foetuses sharing the same womb. Monozygotic twins are genetically identical unless there has been a mutation in development, and they are almost always the same gender.
Dizygotic	Fraternal twins (commonly known as "non-identical twins") usually occur when two fertilized eggs are implanted in the uterine wall at the same time. The two eggs form two zygotes, and these twins are therefore also known as dizygotic.
Gene	A gene is an ultramicroscopic area of the chromosome. It is the smallest physical unit of the DNA molecule that carries a piece of hereditary information.
Normative	The term normative is used to describe the effects of those structures of culture which

Go to **Cram101.com** for the Practice Tests for this Chapter.

	regulate the function of social activity.
Correlation	A statistical technique for determining the degree of association between two or more variables is referred to as correlation.
Obesity	The state of being more than 20 percent above the average weight for a person of one's height is called obesity.
Body mass index	The body mass index is a calculated number, used to compare and analyse the health effects of body weight on human bodies of all heights. It is equal to the weight, divided by the square of the height.
Nervous system	The body's electrochemical communication circuitry, made up of billions of neurons is a nervous system.
Diabetes	Diabetes is a medical disorder characterized by varying or persistent elevated blood sugar levels, especially after eating. All types of diabetes share similar symptoms and complications at advanced stages: dehydration and ketoacidosis, cardiovascular disease, chronic renal failure, retinal damage which can lead to blindness, nerve damage which can lead to erectile dysfunction, gangrene with risk of amputation of toes, feet, and even legs.
Asthma	Asthma is a complex disease characterized by bronchial hyperresponsiveness (BHR), inflammation, mucus production and intermittent airway obstruction.
Stroke	A stroke occurs when the blood supply to a part of the brain is suddenly interrupted by occlusion, by hemorrhage, or other causes
Prenatal	Prenatal period refers to the time from conception to birth.
Fetus	A fetus develops from the end of the 8th week of pregnancy (when the major structures have formed), until birth.
Longitudinal study	Longitudinal study is a type of developmental study in which the same group of participants is followed and measured for an extended period of time, often years.
Maturation	The orderly unfolding of traits, as regulated by the genetic code is called maturation.
Metabolic rate	Metabolic rate refers to the rate at which the body burns calories to produce energy.
Habit	A habit is a response that has become completely separated from its eliciting stimulus. Early learning theorists used the term to describe S-R associations, however not all S-R associations become a habit, rather many are extinguished after reinforcement is withdrawn.
Learning	Learning is a relatively permanent change in behavior that results from experience. Thus, to attribute a behavioral change to learning, the change must be relatively permanent and must result from experience.
Shaping	The concept of reinforcing successive, increasingly accurate approximations to a target behavior is called shaping. The target behavior is broken down into a hierarchy of elemental steps, each step more sophisticated then the last. By successively reinforcing each of the the elemental steps, a form of differential reinforcement, until that step is learned while extinguishing the step below, the target behavior is gradually achieved.
Synapse	A synapse is specialized junction through which cells of the nervous system signal to one another and to non-neuronal cells such as muscles or glands.
Neuron	The neuron is the primary cell of the nervous system. They are found in the brain, the spinal cord, in the nerves and ganglia of the peripheral nervous system. It is a specialized cell that conducts impulses through the nervous system and contains three major parts: cell body, dendrites, and an axon. It can have many dendrites but only one axon.
Frontal lobe	The frontal lobe comprises four major folds of cortical tissue: the precentral gyrus,

	superior gyrus and the middle gyrus of the frontal gyri, the inferior frontal gyrus. It has been found to play a part in impulse control, judgement, language, memory, motor function, problem solving, sexual behavior, socialization and spontaneity.
Lobes	The four major sections of the cerebral cortex: frontal, parietal, temporal, and occipital are called lobes.
Causation	Causation concerns the time order relationship between two or more objects such that if a specific antecendent condition occurs the same consequent must always follow.
Early childhood	Early childhood refers to the developmental period extending from the end of infancy to about 5 or 6 years of age; sometimes called the preschool years.
Script	A schema, or behavioral sequence, for an event is called a script. It is a form of schematic organization, with real-world events organized in terms of temporal and causal relations between component acts.
Cognitive development	The process by which a child's understanding of the world changes as a function of age and experience is called cognitive development.
Piaget	Piaget argued that young children's answers were qualitatively different than older children rather than quantitative. There are two major aspects to his theory: the process of coming to know and the stages we move through as we gradually acquire this ability.
Concrete operations	In Piaget's theory, the third major stage of cognitive development, in which children can decenter their perception, are less egocentric, and can think logically about concrete objects is called concrete operations.
Nerve	A nerve is an enclosed, cable-like bundle of nerve fibers or axons, which includes the glia that ensheath the axons in myelin. Neurons are sometimes called nerve cells, though this term is technically imprecise since many neurons do not form nerves.
Conservation	Conservation refers to the recognition that basic properties of substances such as weight and mass remain the same even when transformations merely alter their appearance.
Compensation	In personaility, compensation, according to Adler, is an effort to overcome imagined or real inferiorities by developing one's abilities.
Reversibility	Reversibility according to Piaget, is recognition that processes can be undone, that things can be made as they were.
Egocentrism	The inability to distinguish between one's own perspective and someone else's is referred to as egocentrism.
Punishment	Punishment is the addtion of a stimulus that reduces the frequency of a response, or the removal of a stimulus that results in a reduction of the response.
Principle of conservation	The knowledge that the quantity of a substance remains the same even though its shape or other aspects of its physical appearance might change is the principle of conservation.
Conservation of number	The knowledge that the number of items in an array remains the same despite changes in the form of the array is referred to as the conservation of number.
Infancy	The developmental period that extends from birth to 18 or 24 months is called infancy.
Working Memory	Working memory is the collection of structures and processes in the brain used for temporarily storing and manipulating information. Working memory consists of both memory for items that are currently being processed, and components governing attention and directing the processing itself.
Memory span	The second key concept associated with a short-term memory is that it has a finite capacity. Prior to the creation of current memory models, George Miller argued that human short-term

	memory has a forward memory span of approximately seven items plus or minus two.
Electrode	Any device used to electrically stimulate nerve tissue or to record its activity is an electrode.
Knowledge base	The general background information a person possesses, which influences most cognitive task performance is called the knowledge base.
Elaboration	The extensiveness of processing at any given level of memory is called elaboration. The use of elaboration changes developmentally. Adolescents are more likely to use elaboration spontaneously than children.
Free recall	In memory research, a task in which a subject recalls information without specific cues or prompts is referred to as free recall.
Metamemory	Metamemory refers to self-awareness of the ways in which memory functions, allowing the person to encode, store, and retrieve information effectively.
Psychological test	Psychological test refers to a standardized measure of a sample of a person's behavior.
Stages	Stages represent relatively discrete periods of time in which functioning is qualitatively different from functioning at other periods.
Problem solving	An attempt to find an appropriate way of attaining a goal when the goal is not readily available is called problem solving.
Cognition	The intellectual processes through which information is obtained, transformed, stored, retrieved, and otherwise used is cognition.
Evolution	Commonly used to refer to gradual change, evolution is the change in the frequency of alleles within a population from one generation to the next. This change may be caused by different mechanisms, including natural selection, genetic drift, or changes in population (gene flow).
Blocking	If the one of the two members of a compound stimulus fails to produce the CR due to an earlier conditioning of the other member of the compound stimulus, blocking has occurred.
Reliability	Reliability means the extent to which a test produces a consistent , reproducible score .
Tower of Hanoi	The Tower of Hanoi is a mathematical game or puzzle. It consists of three pegs, and a number of discs of different sizes which can slot onto any peg. It is used to study problem-solving behavior.
Metacognition	Metacognition refers to thinking about cognition (memory, perception, calculation, association, etc.) itself. Metacognition can be divided into two types of knowledge: explicit, conscious, factual knowledge; and implicit, unconscious, procedural knowledge.
Inference	Inference is the act or process of drawing a conclusion based solely on what one already knows.
Superordinate	A hypernym is a word whose extension includes the extension of the word of which it is a hypernym. A word that is more generic or broad than another given word. Another term for a hypernym is a superordinate.
Feedback	Feedback refers to information returned to a person about the effects a response has had.
Mental processes	The thoughts, feelings, and motives that each of us experiences privately but that cannot be observed directly are called mental processes.
Reasoning	Reasoning is the act of using reason to derive a conclusion from certain premises. There are two main methods to reach a conclusion,deductive reasoning and inductive reasoning.
Concrete	According to Piaget, the period from 7 to 12 years of age, which is characterized by logical

Go to **Cram101.com** for the Practice Tests for this Chapter.

operational	thought and a loss of egocentrism, is referred to as concrete operational stage. Conservation skills are formed - understanding that quantity, length or number of items is unrelated to the appearance of the object or items.
Clustering	Clustering is a technique used to enhance the memory by organization of conceptually-related categories.
Analogy	An analogy is a comparison between two different things, in order to highlight some form of similarity. Analogy is the cognitive process of transferring information from a particular subject to another particular subject.
Cultural values	The importance and desirability of various objects and activities as defined by people in a given culture are referred to as cultural values.
Sternberg	Sternberg proposed the triarchic theory of intelligence: componential, experiential, and practical. His notion of general intelligence or the g-factor, is a composite of intelligence scores across multiple modalities.
Myelination	The process in which the nerve cells are covered and insulated with a layer of fat cells, which increases the speed at which information travels through the nervous system is referred to as myelination.

Ecstasy	Ecstasy as an emotion is to be outside oneself, in a trancelike state in which an individual transcends ordinary consciousness and as a result has a heightened capacity for exceptional thought or experience. Ecstasy also refers to a relatively new hallucinogen that is chemically similar to mescaline and the amphetamines.
Learning	Learning is a relatively permanent change in behavior that results from experience. Thus, to attribute a behavioral change to learning, the change must be relatively permanent and must result from experience.
Society	The social sciences use the term society to mean a group of people that form a semi-closed (or semi-open) social system, in which most interactions are with other individuals belonging to the group.
Socialization	Social rules and social relations are created, communicated, and changed in verbal and nonverbal ways creating social complexity useful in identifying outsiders and intelligent breeding partners. The process of learning these skills is called socialization.
Acquisition	Acquisition is the process of adapting to the environment, learning or becoming conditioned. In classical conditoning terms, it is the initial learning of the stimulus response link, which involves a neutral stimulus being associated with a unconditioned stimulus and becoming a conditioned stimulus.
Bruner	Bruner has had an enormous impact on educational psychology with his contributions to cognitive learning theory. His ideas are based on categorization, maintaining that people interpret the world in terms of its similarities and differences.
Motivation	In psychology, motivation is the driving force (desire) behind all actions of an organism.
Infancy	The developmental period that extends from birth to 18 or 24 months is called infancy.
Punishment	Punishment is the addtion of a stimulus that reduces the frequency of a response, or the removal of a stimulus that results in a reduction of the response.
Phoneme	In oral language, a phoneme is the theoretical basic unit of sound that can be used to distinguish words or morphemes; in sign language, it is a similarly basic unit of hand shape, motion, position, or facial expression.
Decoding	Process of phonetic analysis by which a printed word is converted to spoken form before retrieval from long-term memory is called decoding.
Phonemic awareness	Phonemic Awareness is a subset of Phonological Awareness in which listeners are able to distinguish phonemes, the smallest units of sound.
Problem solving	An attempt to find an appropriate way of attaining a goal when the goal is not readily available is called problem solving.
Microgenetic	A design that allows researchers to directly observe change by repeated testing over a relatively short time period is called a microgenetic study. The idea is to study change as change is occurring.
Feedback	Feedback refers to information returned to a person about the effects a response has had.
Reciprocal teaching	In reciprocal teaching, students taking turns leading a small-group discussion.
Script	A schema, or behavioral sequence, for an event is called a script. It is a form of schematic organization, with real-world events organized in terms of temporal and causal relations between component acts.
Ann Brown	Ann Brown developed the method of reciprocal teaching, in which teachers and students take turns leading structured discussions of text.

Zone of proximal development	The zone of proximal development is the gap between a learner's current or actual level of development determined by independent problem solving and the learner's emerging or potential level of development. Learners cannot build new knowledge without first having a framework or prior learning foundation.
Proximal	Students can set both long-term (distal) and short-term (proximal) goals .
Aristotle	Aristotle can be credited with the development of the first theory of learning. He concluded that ideas were generated in consciousness based on four principlesof association: contiguity, similarity, contrast, and succession. In contrast to Plato, he believed that knowledge derived from sensory experience and was not inherited.
Pupil	In the eye, the pupil is the opening in the middle of the iris. It appears black because most of the light entering it is absorbed by the tissues inside the eye. The size of the pupil is controlled by involuntary contraction and dilation of the iris, in order to regulate the intensity of light entering the eye. This is known as the pupillary reflex.
Construct	A generalized concept, such as anxiety or gravity, is a construct.
Piaget	Piaget argued that young children's answers were qualitatively different than older children rather than quantitative. There are two major aspects to his theory: the process of coming to know and the stages we move through as we gradually acquire this ability.
Norms	In testing, standards of test performance that permit the comparison of one person's score on the test to the scores of others who have taken the same test are referred to as norms.
Reasoning	Reasoning is the act of using reason to derive a conclusion from certain premises. There are two main methods to reach a conclusion,deductive reasoning and inductive reasoning.
Research design	A research design tests a hypothesis. The basic typess are: descriptive, correlational, and experimental.
Affect	A subjective feeling or emotional tone often accompanied by bodily expressions noticeable to others is called affect.
Conservation	Conservation refers to the recognition that basic properties of substances such as weight and mass remain the same even when transformations merely alter their appearance.
Concrete operational	According to Piaget, the period from 7 to 12 years of age, which is characterized by logical thought and a loss of egocentrism, is referred to as concrete operational stage. Conservation skills are formed - understanding that quantity, length or number of items is unrelated to the appearance of the object or items.
Infant mortality	Infant mortality is the death of infants in the first year of life. The leading causes of infant mortality are dehydration and disease. Major causes of infant mortality in more developed countries include congenital malformation, infection and SIDS. Infant mortality rate is the number of newborns dying under a year of age divided by the number of live births during the year.
Habit	A habit is a response that has become completely separated from its eliciting stimulus. Early learning theorists used the term to describe S-R associations, however not all S-R associations become a habit, rather many are extinguished after reinforcement is withdrawn.
Direct observation	Direct observation refers to assessing behavior through direct surveillance.
Knowledge base	The general background information a person possesses, which influences most cognitive task performance is called the knowledge base.
Attitude	An enduring mental representation of a person, place, or thing that evokes an emotional response and related behavior is called attitude.

Go to **Cram101.com** for the Practice Tests for this Chapter.

Developmental psychologist	A psychologist interested in human growth and development from conception until death is referred to as a developmental psychologist.
Individual differences	Individual differences psychology studies the ways in which individual people differ in their behavior. This is distinguished from other aspects of psychology in that although psychology is ostensibly a study of individuals, modern psychologists invariably study groups.
Obedience	Obedience is the willingness to follow the will of others. Humans have been shown to be surprisingly obedient in the presence of perceived legitimate authority figures, as demonstrated by the Milgram experiment in the 1960s.
Intelligence test	An intelligence test is a standardized means of assessing a person's current mental ability, for example, the Stanford-Binet test and the Wechsler Adult Intelligence Scale.
Validity	The extent to which a test measures what it is intended to measure is called validity.
Attention	Attention is the cognitive process of selectively concentrating on one thing while ignoring other things. Psychologists have labeled three types of attention: sustained attention, selective attention, and divided attention.
Nurture	Nurture refers to the environmental influences on behavior due to nutrition, culture, socioeconomic status, and learning.
William Stern	William Stern developed the original formula for the Intelligence Quotient (IQ) after studying the scores on Binet's intelligence test.
Mental age	The mental age refers to the accumulated months of credit that a person earns on the Stanford-Binet Intelligence Scale.
Wechsler	Wechsler is best known for his intelligence tests. The Wechsler Adult Intelligence Scale (WAIS) was developed first in 1939 and then called the Wechsler-Bellevue Intelligence Test. From these he derived the Wechsler Intelligence Scale for Children (WISC) in 1949 and the Wechsler Preschool and Primary Scale of Intelligence (WPPSI) in 1967. Wechsler originally created these tests to find out more about his patients at the Bellevue clinic and he found the then-current Binet IQ test unsatisfactory.
Normal distribution	A normal distribution is a symmetrical distribution of scores that is assumed to reflect chance fluctuations; approximately 68% of cases lie within a single standard deviation of the mean.
Raw score	A raw score is an original datum that has not been transformed – for example, the original result obtained by a student on a test (i.e., the number of correctly answered items) as opposed to that score after transformation to a standard score or percentile rank or the like.
Intelligence quotient	An intelligence quotient is a score derived from a set of standardized tests that were developed with the purpose of measuring a person's cognitive abilities ("intelligence") in relation to their age group.
Chronological age	Chronological age refers to the number of years that have elapsed since a person's birth.
IQ test	An IQ test is a standardized test developed to measure a person's cognitive abilities ("intelligence") in relation to their age group.
Charles Spearman	Charles Spearman is known for his work in statistics, as a pioneer of factor analysis, and for his rank correlation coefficient. He also did seminal work on models for human intelligence, including discovering that disparate cognitive test scores reflect a single general factor and coining the term g factor.
Correlation	A statistical technique for determining the degree of association between two or more

variables is referred to as correlation.

Mackintosh	Mackintosh argues that in blocking, participants do learn something about the redundant cue in the compound stimulus. Specifically, participants learn to suppress attention to it because it predicts no change in reinforcement. This theory asserts that blocking is not caused solely by lack of learning, but by learned inattention to the blocked cue.
Arthur Jensen	Arthur Jensen was a major practitioner of individual differences psychology with a special interest in intelligence and the nature versus nurture debate, and argued strongly that intelligence is partially heritable.
Positive correlation	A relationship between two variables in which both vary in the same direction is called a positive correlation.
Innate	Innate behavior is not learned or influenced by the environment, rather, it is present or predisposed at birth.
Brain	The brain controls and coordinates most movement, behavior and homeostatic body functions such as heartbeat, blood pressure, fluid balance and body temperature. Functions of the brain are responsible for cognition, emotion, memory, motor learning and other sorts of learning. The brain is primarily made up of two types of cells: glia and neurons.
Triarchic Theory of Intelligence	The Triarchic Theory of Intelligence was formulated by Robert J. Sternberg. It proposes that intelligence consists of componential intelligence, experiential intelligence, and contextual intelligence.
Triarchic theory	Sternberg's theory that there are three main types of intelligence: analytical, creative, and practical is called the triarchic theory of intelligence.
Sternberg	Sternberg proposed the triarchic theory of intelligence: componential, experiential, and practical. His notion of general intelligence or the g-factor, is a composite of intelligence scores across multiple modalities.
Population	Population refers to all members of a well-defined group of organisms, events, or things.
Yerkes	Yerkes worked in the field of comparative psychology. He is best known for studying the intelligence and social behavior of gorillas and chimpanzees. Joining with John D. Dodson, he developed the Yerkes-Dodson law relating arousal to performance.
Moron	Moron, was originally a scientific term, coined by psychologist Henry Goddard from a Greek word meaning "foolish", and used to describe a person with a genetically determined mental age between 8 and 12 on the Binet scale.
Hypothesis	A specific statement about behavior or mental processes that is testable through research is a hypothesis.
Mental retardation	Mental retardation refers to having significantly below-average intellectual functioning and limitations in at least two areas of adaptive functioning. Many categorize retardation as mild, moderate, severe, or profound.
Phenotype	The phenotype of an individual organism is either its total physical appearance and constitution, or a specific manifestation of a trait, such as size or eye color, that varies between individuals. Phenotype is determined to some extent by genotype, or by the identity of the alleles that an individual carries at one or more positions on the chromosomes.
Monozygotic	Identical twins occur when a single egg is fertilized to form one zygote, calld monozygotic, but the zygote then divides into two separate embryos. The two embryos develop into foetuses sharing the same womb. Monozygotic twins are genetically identical unless there has been a mutation in development, and they are almost always the same gender.
Identical twins	Identical twins occur when a single egg is fertilized to form one zygote (monozygotic) but

Go to **Cram101.com** for the Practice Tests for this Chapter.

	the zygote then divides into two separate embryos. The two embryos develop into foetuses sharing the same womb. Monozygotic twins are genetically identical unless there has been a mutation in development, and they are almost always the same gender.
Fraternal twins	Fraternal twins usually occur when two fertilized eggs are implanted in the uterine wall at the same time. The two eggs form two zygotes, and these twins are therefore also known as dizygotic. Dizygotic twins are no more similar genetically than any siblings.
Twin study	A twin study is a kind of genetic study done to determine heritability. The premise is that since identical twins (especially identical twins raised apart) have identical genotypes, differences between them are solely due to environmental factors. By examining the degree to which twins are differentiated, a study may determine the extent to which a particular trait is influenced by genes or the environment.
Bronfenbrenner	Bronfenbrenner was a co-founder of the U.S. national Head Start program and founder of the Ecological Theory of Development.
Heritability	Heritability It is that proportion of the observed variation in a particular phenotype within a particular population, that can be attributed to the contribution of genotype. In other words: it measures the extent to which differences between individuals in a population are due their being different genetically.
Ethnic group	An ethnic group is a culture or subculture whose members are readily distinguishable by outsiders based on traits originating from a common racial, national, linguistic, or religious source. Members of an ethnic group are often presumed to be culturally or biologically similar, although this is not in fact necessarily the case.
Herrnstein	Herrnstein was a prominent researcher in comparative psychology who did pioneering work on pigeon intelligence employing the Experimental Analysis of Behavior and formulated the "Matching Law" in the 1960s, a breakthrough in understanding how reinforcement and behavior are linked.
Empirical	Empirical means the use of working hypotheses which are capable of being disproved using observation or experiment.
Statistic	A statistic is an observable random variable of a sample.
Ethnicity	Ethnicity refers to a characteristic based on cultural heritage, nationality characteristics, race, religion, and language.
Learning disability	A learning disability exists when there is a significant discrepancy between one's ability and achievement.
Quantitative	A quantitative property is one that exists in a range of magnitudes, and can therefore be measured. Measurements of any particular quantitative property are expressed as as a specific quantity, referred to as a unit, multiplied by a number.
Dyslexia	Dyslexia is a neurological disorder with biochemical and genetic markers. In its most common and apparent form, it is a disability in which a person's reading and/or writing ability is significantly lower than that which would be predicted by his or her general level of intelligence.
Standardized test	An oral or written assessment for which an individual receives a score indicating how the individual reponded relative to a previously tested large sample of others is referred to as a standardized test.
Theories	Theories are logically self-consistent models or frameworks describing the behavior of a certain natural or social phenomenon. They are broad explanations and predictions concerning phenomena of interest.

Go to **Cram101.com** for the Practice Tests for this Chapter.

Brightness	The dimension of visual sensation that is dependent on the intensity of light reflected from a surface and that corresponds to the amplitude of the light wave is called brightness.
Visual cortex	The visual cortex is the general term applied to both the primary visual cortex and the visual association area. Anatomically, the visual cortex occupies the entire occipital lobe, the inferior temporal lobe (IT), posterior parts of the parietal lobe, and a few small regions in the frontal lobe.
Discrimination	In Learning theory, discrimination refers the ability to distinguish between a conditioned stimulus and other stimuli. It can be brought about by extensive training or differential reinforcement. In social terms, it is the denial of privileges to a person or a group on the basis of prejudice.
Incentive	An incentive is what is expected once a behavior is performed. An incentive acts as a reinforcer.
Eccles	Eccles was key to a number of important developments in neuroscience. Until around 1949, Eccles believed that synaptic transmission was primarily electrical rather than chemical. Although he was wrong in this hypothesis, his arguments led himself and others to perform some of the experiments which proved chemical synaptic transmission.
Mastery orientation	According to Dweck, mastery orientation is an outlook in which individuals focus on the task rather than on their ability, have positive affect, and generate solution-oriented strategies that improve their performance.
Performance orientation	Performance orientation is an outlook in which individuals are concerned with performance outcome rather than performance process. For performance-oriented students, winning is what matters.
Insight	Insight refers to a sudden awareness of the relationships among various elements that had previously appeared to be independent of one another.
Interdependence	Interdependence is a dynamic of being mutually responsible to and dependent on others.
Individualistic	Cultures have been classified as individualistic, which means having a set of values that give priority to personal goals rather than group goals.
Wisdom	Wisdom is the ability to make correct judgments and decisions. It is an intangible quality gained through experience. Whether or not something is wise is determined in a pragmatic sense by its popularity, how long it has been around, and its ability to predict against future events.
Cultural values	The importance and desirability of various objects and activities as defined by people in a given culture are referred to as cultural values.
Ethnographic study	Ethnographic study is an in-depth study of a culture, which uses a combination of methods including participant observation.
Inference	Inference is the act or process of drawing a conclusion based solely on what one already knows.
Social class	Social class describes the relationships between people in hierarchical societies or cultures. Those with more power usually subordinate those with less power.
Cognitive development	The process by which a child's understanding of the world changes as a function of age and experience is called cognitive development.
Motives	Needs or desires that energize and direct behavior toward a goal are motives.
Cognitive skills	Cognitive skills such as reasoning, attention, and memory can be advanced and sustained through practice and training.

| **Metacognition** | Metacognition refers to thinking about cognition (memory, perception, calculation, association, etc.) itself. Metacognition can be divided into two types of knowledge: explicit, conscious, factual knowledge; and implicit, unconscious, procedural knowledge. |

Reasoning	Reasoning is the act of using reason to derive a conclusion from certain premises. There are two main methods to reach a conclusion, deductive reasoning and inductive reasoning.
Theories	Theories are logically self-consistent models or frameworks describing the behavior of a certain natural or social phenomenon. They are broad explanations and predictions concerning phenomena of interest.
Friendship	The essentials of friendship are reciprocity and commitment between individuals who see themselves more or less as equals. Interaction between friends rests on a more equal power base than the interaction between children and adults.
Society	The social sciences use the term society to mean a group of people that form a semi-closed (or semi-open) social system, in which most interactions are with other individuals belonging to the group.
Social role	Social role refers to expected behavior patterns associated with particular social positions.
Obedience	Obedience is the willingness to follow the will of others. Humans have been shown to be surprisingly obedient in the presence of perceived legitimate authority figures, as demonstrated by the Milgram experiment in the 1960s.
Research method	The scope of the research method is to produce some new knowledge. This, in principle, can take three main forms: Exploratory research; Constructive research; and Empirical research.
Piaget	Piaget argued that young children's answers were qualitatively different than older children rather than quantitative. There are two major aspects to his theory: the process of coming to know and the stages we move through as we gradually acquire this ability.
Projection	Attributing one's own undesirable thoughts, impulses, traits, or behaviors to others is referred to as projection.
Adolescence	The period of life bounded by puberty and the assumption of adult responsibilities is adolescence.
Attention	Attention is the cognitive process of selectively concentrating on one thing while ignoring other things. Psychologists have labeled three types of attention: sustained attention, selective attention, and divided attention.
Concrete operational	According to Piaget, the period from 7 to 12 years of age, which is characterized by logical thought and a loss of egocentrism, is referred to as concrete operational stage. Conservation skills are formed - understanding that quantity, length or number of items is unrelated to the appearance of the object or items.
Early childhood	Early childhood refers to the developmental period extending from the end of infancy to about 5 or 6 years of age; sometimes called the preschool years.
Social development	The person's developing capacity for social relationships and the effects of those relationships on further development is referred to as social development.
Hartup	According to Hartup, the single best childhood predictor of adult adaptation is not school grades, and not classroom behavior, but rather, the adequacy with which the child gets along with other children.
Pretend play	According to Piaget and Smilansky, pretend play is the third cognitive level of play. It involves imaginary people or situations.
Script	A schema, or behavioral sequence, for an event is called a script. It is a form of schematic organization, with real-world events organized in terms of temporal and causal relations between component acts.
Acquisition	Acquisition is the process of adapting to the environment, learning or becoming conditioned.

	In classical conditoning terms, it is the initial learning of the stimulus response link, which involves a neutral stimulus being associated with a unconditioned stimulus and becoming a conditioned stimulus.
Trait	An enduring personality characteristic that tends to lead to certain behaviors is called a trait. The term trait also means a genetically inherited feature of an organism.
Moral development	Development regarding rules and conventions about what people should do in their interactions with other people is called moral development.
Psychoanalytic	Freud's theory that unconscious forces act as determinants of personality is called psychoanalytic theory. The theory is a developmental theory characterized by critical stages of development.
Superego	Frued's third psychic structure, which functions as a moral guardian and sets forth high standards for behavior is the superego.
Psychoanalytic theory	Psychoanalytic theory is a general term for approaches to psychoanalysis which attempt to provide a conceptual framework more-or-less independent of clinical practice rather than based on empirical analysis of clinical cases.
Personality	Personality refers to the pattern of enduring characteristics that differentiates a person, the patterns of behaviors that make each individual unique.
Internalization	The developmental change from behavior that is externally controlled to behavior that is controlled by internal standards and principles is referred to as internalization.
Moral judgment	Making decisions about which actions are right and which are wrong is a moral judgment.
Kohlberg	Kohlberg believed that people progressed in their moral reasoning through a series of developmental stages.
Moral reasoning	Moral reasoning involves concepts of justice, whereas social conventional judgments are concepts of social organization.
Heteronomous	From his observations, Piaget concluded that children begin in a heteronomous stage of moral reasoning, characterized by a strict adherence to rules and duties, and obedience to authority.
Stages	Stages represent relatively discrete periods of time in which functioning is qualitatively different from functioning at other periods.
Punishment	Punishment is the addtion of a stimulus that reduces the frequency of a response, or the removal of a stimulus that results in a reduction of the response.
Individualistic	Cultures have been classified as individualistic, which means having a set of values that give priority to personal goals rather than group goals.
Motives	Needs or desires that energize and direct behavior toward a goal are motives.
Validity	The extent to which a test measures what it is intended to measure is called validity.
Social norm	A social norm, is a rule that is socially enforced. In social situations, such as meetings, they are unwritten and often unstated rules that govern individuals' behavior. A social norm is most evident when not followed or broken.
Empathy	Empathy is the recognition and understanding of the states of mind, including beliefs, desires and particularly emotions of others without injecting your own.
Norms	In testing, standards of test performance that permit the comparison of one person's score on the test to the scores of others who have taken the same test are referred to as norms.
Survey	A method of scientific investigation in which a large sample of people answer questions about

their attitudes or behavior is referred to as a survey.

Developmental psychologist	A psychologist interested in human growth and development from conception until death is referred to as a developmental psychologist.
Relational aggression	Relational Aggression usually stems from miscommunication and the unsynchronisation of feelings between the partners. The unspoken tension between partners in this kind of problematic relationship tends to manifest itself in aggression towards the partner in subtle, but potentially devastating mannerisms.
Species	Species refers to a reproductively isolated breeding population.
Longitudinal study	Longitudinal study is a type of developmental study in which the same group of participants is followed and measured for an extended period of time, often years.
Social skills	Social skills are skills used to interact and communicate with others to assist status in the social structure and other motivations.
Chronic	Chronic refers to a relatively long duration, usually more than a few months.
Tics	Tics are a repeated, impulsive action, almost reflexive in nature, which the person feels powerless to control or avoid.
Rejected children	Children who are infrequently nominated as a best friend and are actively disliked by their peers are referred to as rejected children.
Neglected children	Neglected children are infrequently nominated as a best friend but are not disliked by their peers.
Controversial children	Controversial children are frequently nominated both as one's best friend and as being disliked by peers.
Physical attractiveness	Physical attractiveness is the perception of an individual as physically beautiful by other people.
Sociometric status	A sociometric status is used to describe the extent to which children are liked or disliked by their peer group. Sociometric status is typically assessed by asking children to rate how much they like or dislike each of their classmates.
Positive relationship	Statistically, a positive relationship refers to a mathematical relationship in which increases in one measure are matched by increases in the other.
Popular children	Children who are frequently nominated as a best friend and are rarely disliked by their peers are called popular children.
Questionnaire	A self-report method of data collection or clinical assessment method in which the individual being studied checks off items on a printed list, answers multiple-choice questions, or writes out answers to essay questions aimed at producing a selfdescription is called questionnaire.
Social comparison	Social comparison theory is the idea that individuals learn about and assess themselves by comparison with other people. Research shows that individuals tend to lean more toward social comparisons in situations that are ambiguous.
Problem solving	An attempt to find an appropriate way of attaining a goal when the goal is not readily available is called problem solving.
Affect	A subjective feeling or emotional tone often accompanied by bodily expressions noticeable to others is called affect.
Prospective study	Prospective study is a long-term study of a group of people, beginning before the onset of a common disorder. It allows investigators to see how the disorder develops.

Retrospective study	A retrospective study looks at past behavior, while a prospective study looks at future behavior.
Hypothesis	A specific statement about behavior or mental processes that is testable through research is a hypothesis.
Longitudinal approach	The Longitudinal approach is a research strategy in which the same individuals are studied over a period of time, usually several years or more.
Representative sample	Representative sample refers to a sample of participants selected from the larger population in such a way that important subgroups within the population are included in the sample in the same proportions as they are found in the larger population.
Kagan	The work of Kagan supports the concept of an inborn, biologically based temperamental predisposition to severe anxiety.
Kibbutz	Kibbutz is an Israeli farming community in which children are reared in group settings.
Predisposition	Predisposition refers to an inclination or diathesis to respond in a certain way, either inborn or acquired. In abnormal psychology, it is a factor that lowers the ability to withstand stress and inclines the individual toward pathology.
Interdependence	Interdependence is a dynamic of being mutually responsible to and dependent on others.
Learning	Learning is a relatively permanent change in behavior that results from experience. Thus, to attribute a behavioral change to learning, the change must be relatively permanent and must result from experience.
Cooperative learning	Cooperative learning was proposed in response to traditional curriculum-driven education. In cooperative learning environments, students interact in purposively structured heterogenous group to support the learning of one self and others in the same group.
Reflection	Reflection is the process of rephrasing or repeating thoughts and feelings expressed, making the person more aware of what they are saying or thinking.
Cultural values	The importance and desirability of various objects and activities as defined by people in a given culture are referred to as cultural values.
Graham	Graham has conducted a number of studies that reveal stronger socioeconomic-status influences rather than ethnic influences in achievement.
Counselor	A counselor is a mental health professional who specializes in helping people with problems not involving serious mental disorders.
Generalization	In conditioning, the tendency for a conditioned response to be evoked by stimuli that are similar to the stimulus to which the response was conditioned is a generalization. The greater the similarity among the stimuli, the greater the probability of generalization.
Ethnographic study	Ethnographic study is an in-depth study of a culture, which uses a combination of methods including participant observation.
Sullivan	Sullivan developed the Self System, a configuration of the personality traits developed in childhood and reinforced by positive affirmation and the security operations developed in childhood to avoid anxiety and threats to self-esteem.
Developmental level	An individual's current state of physical, emotional, and intellectual development is called the developmental level.
Perspective taking	Perspective taking refers to the ability to assume another person's perspective and understand his or her thoughts and feelings. An adolescent can step outside a two-person interchange and view the interaction from a third-person perspective; younger children cannot.

Egocentrism	The inability to distinguish between one's own perspective and someone else's is referred to as egocentrism.
Autonomy	Autonomy is the condition of something that does not depend on anything else.
Coregulation	A gradual transferring of control from parent to child, beginning in middle childhood is referred to as coregulation.
Attachment	Attachment is the tendency to seek closeness to another person and feel secure when that person is present.
Bias	A bias is a prejudice in a general or specific sense, usually in the sense for having a preference to one particular point of view or ideological perspective.
Socialization	Social rules and social relations are created, communicated, and changed in verbal and nonverbal ways creating social complexity useful in identifying outsiders and intelligent breeding partners. The process of learning these skills is called socialization.
Socioeconomic	Socioeconomic pertains to the study of the social and economic impacts of any product or service offering, market intervention or other activity on an economy as a whole and on the companies, organization and individuals who are its main economic actors.
Maladjustment	Maladjustment is the condition of being unable to adapt properly to your environment with resulting emotional instability.
Anxiety	Anxiety is a complex combination of the feeling of fear, apprehension and worry often accompanied by physical sensations such as palpitations, chest pain and/or shortness of breath.
Ethnic group	An ethnic group is a culture or subculture whose members are readily distinguishable by outsiders based on traits originating from a common racial, national, linguistic, or religious source. Members of an ethnic group are often presumed to be culturally or biologically similar, although this is not in fact necessarily the case.
Authoritative parenting	Authoritative parenting encourages children to be independent but still places limits and controls on their actions. Extensive verbal give-and-take is allowed, and parents are warm and nurturant toward the child.
Empirical	Empirical means the use of working hypotheses which are capable of being disproved using observation or experiment.
Shaping	The concept of reinforcing successive, increasingly accurate approximations to a target behavior is called shaping. The target behavior is broken down into a hierarchy of elemental steps, each step more sophisticated then the last. By successively reinforcing each of the the elemental steps, a form of differential reinforcement, until that step is learned while extinguishing the step below, the target behavior is gradually achieved.
Physical proximity	Physical proximity refers to one's actual physical nearness to others in terms of housing, work, school, and so forth.
Individuality	According to Cooper, individuality consists of two dimensions: self-assertion and separateness.
Puberty	Puberty refers to the process of physical changes by which a child's body becomes an adult body capable of reproduction.

Adolescence	The period of life bounded by puberty and the assumption of adult responsibilities is adolescence.
Cultural values	The importance and desirability of various objects and activities as defined by people in a given culture are referred to as cultural values.
Social development	The person's developing capacity for social relationships and the effects of those relationships on further development is referred to as social development.
Direct observation	Direct observation refers to assessing behavior through direct surveillance.
Society	The social sciences use the term society to mean a group of people that form a semi-closed (or semi-open) social system, in which most interactions are with other individuals belonging to the group.
Puberty	Puberty refers to the process of physical changes by which a child's body becomes an adult body capable of reproduction.
Aristotle	Aristotle can be credited with the development of the first theory of learning. He concluded that ideas were generated in consciousness based on four principlesof association: contiguity, similarity, contrast, and succession. In contrast to Plato, he believed that knowledge derived from sensory experience and was not inherited.
Plato	According to Plato, people must come equipped with most of their knowledge and need only hints and contemplation to complete it. Plato suggested that the brain is the mechanism of mental processes and that one gained knowledge by reflecting on the contents of one's mind.
Suicide	Suicide behavior is rare in childhood but escalates in adolescence. The suicide rate increases in a linear fashion from adolescence through late adulthood.
Emotion	An emotion is a mental states that arise spontaneously, rather than through conscious effort. They are often accompanied by physiological changes.
Rousseau	Rousseau rejected the idea of the blank slate. He believed that learning was a natural consequence of human existence. Further, he thought socialization unimportant in development. Because of his insistence that childhood was different than adulthood and his creation of stages of development, he is known as the father of developmental psychology.
Maturation	The orderly unfolding of traits, as regulated by the genetic code is called maturation.
Hull	Hull is best known for the Drive Reduction Theory which postulated that behavior occurs in response to primary drives such as hunger, thirst, sexual interest, etc. When the goal of the drive is attained the drive is reduced. This reduction of drive serves as a reinforcer for learning.
Psychopathology	Psychopathology refers to the field concerned with the nature and development of mental disorders.
Sigmund Freud	Sigmund Freud was the founder of the psychoanalytic school, based on his theory that unconscious motives control much behavior, that particular kinds of unconscious thoughts and memories are the source of neurosis, and that neurosis could be treated through bringing these unconscious thoughts and memories to consciousness in psychoanalytic treatment.
Stanley Hall	His laboratory at Johns Hopkins is considered to be the first American laboratory of psychology. In 1887 Stanley Hall founded the American Journal of Psychology. His interests centered around child development and evolutionary theory
Psychoanalytic	Freud's theory that unconscious forces act as determinants of personality is called psychoanalytic theory. The theory is a developmental theory characterized by critical stages of development.

Go to Cram101.com for the Practice Tests for this Chapter.

Psychoanalytic theory	Psychoanalytic theory is a general term for approaches to psychoanalysis which attempt to provide a conceptual framework more-or-less independent of clinical practice rather than based on empirical analysis of clinical cases.
Personality	Personality refers to the pattern of enduring characteristics that differentiates a person, the patterns of behaviors that make each individual unique.
Instinct	Instinct is the word used to describe inherent dispositions towards particular actions. They are generally an inherited pattern of responses or reactions to certain kinds of situations.
Superego	Frued's third psychic structure, which functions as a moral guardian and sets forth high standards for behavior is the superego.
Ego	In Freud's view the Ego serves to balance our primitive needs and our moral beliefs and taboos. Relying on experience, a healthy Ego provides the ability to adapt to reality and interact with the outside world.
Species	Species refers to a reproductively isolated breeding population.
Early childhood	Early childhood refers to the developmental period extending from the end of infancy to about 5 or 6 years of age; sometimes called the preschool years.
Theories	Theories are logically self-consistent models or frameworks describing the behavior of a certain natural or social phenomenon. They are broad explanations and predictions concerning phenomena of interest.
Rite of passage	A rite of passage is a ritual that marks a change in a person's social or sexual status. The term was popularized by the French ethnographer Arnold van Gennep (1873-1957), in the early part of the twentieth century.
Sexual reproduction	Sexual reproduction is a biological process by which organisms create descendants through the combination of genetic material taken randomly and independently from two different members of the species.
Gland	A gland is an organ in an animal's body that synthesizes a substance for release such as hormones, often into the bloodstream or into cavities inside the body or its outer surface.
Pituitary gland	The pituitary gland is an endocrine gland about the size of a pea that sits in the small, bony cavity at the base of the brain. The pituitary gland secretes hormones regulating a wide variety of bodily activities, including trophic hormones that stimulate other endocrine glands.
Growth hormone	Growth hormone is a polypeptide hormone synthesised and secreted by the anterior pituitary gland which stimulates growth and cell reproduction in humans and other vertebrate animals.
Hypothalamus	The hypothalamus is a region of the brain located below the thalamus, forming the major portion of the ventral region of the diencephalon and functioning to regulate certain metabolic processes and other autonomic activities.
Hormone	A hormone is a chemical messenger from one cell (or group of cells) to another. The best known are those produced by endocrine glands, but they are produced by nearly every organ system. The function of hormones is to serve as a signal to the target cells; the action of the hormone is determined by the pattern of secretion and the signal transduction of the receiving tissue.
Progesterone	A female sex hormone that promotes growth of the sex organs and helps maintain pregnancy is called progesterone.
Estrogen	Estrogen is a group of steroid compounds that function as the primary female sex hormone. They are produced primarily by developing follicles in the ovaries, the corpus luteum and the placenta.

Ovary	The female reproductive organ is the ovary. It performs two major functions: producing eggs and secreting hormones.
Testosterone	Testosterone is a steroid hormone from the androgen group. It is the principal male sex hormone and the "original" anabolic steroid.
Testes	Testes are the male reproductive glands or gonads; this is where sperm develop and are stored.
Asynchronous growth	Asynchronous growth is imbalanced growth, a characteristic of adolescence.
Gonads	The gonads are the organs that make gametes. Gametes are haploid germ cells. For example, sperm and egg cells are gametes. In the male the gonads are the testicles, and in the female the gonads are the ovaries.
Gray matter	Gray matter is a category of nervous tissue with many nerve cell bodies and few myelinated axons. Generally, gray matter can be understood as the parts of the brain responsible for information processing; whereas, white matter is responsible for information transmission. In addition, gray matter does not have a myelin sheath and does not regenerate after injury unlike white matter.
Brain	The brain controls and coordinates most movement, behavior and homeostatic body functions such as heartbeat, blood pressure, fluid balance and body temperature. Functions of the brain are responsible for cognition, emotion, memory, motor learning and other sorts of learning. The brain is primarily made up of two types of cells: glia and neurons.
White matter	White matter is one of the two main solid components of the central nervous system. It is composed of axons which connect various grey matter areas of the brain to each other and carry nerve impulses between neurons.
Lungs	The lungs are the essential organs of respiration. Its principal function is to transport oxygen from the atmosphere into the bloodstream, and excrete carbon dioxide from the bloodstream into the atmosphere.
Frontal lobe	The frontal lobe comprises four major folds of cortical tissue: the precentral gyrus, superior gyrus and the middle gyrus of the frontal gyri, the inferior frontal gyrus. It has been found to play a part in impulse control, judgement, language, memory, motor function, problem solving, sexual behavior, socialization and spontaneity.
Lobes	The four major sections of the cerebral cortex: frontal, parietal, temporal, and occipital are called lobes.
Longitudinal study	Longitudinal study is a type of developmental study in which the same group of participants is followed and measured for an extended period of time, often years.
Neocortex	The neocortex is part of the cerebral cortex which covers most of the surface of the cerebral hemispheres including the frontal, parietal, occipital, and temporal lobes. Often seen as the hallmark of human intelligence, the role of this structure in the brain appears to be involved in conscious thought, spatial reasoning, and sensory perception.
Myelin	Myelin is an electrically insulating fatty layer that surrounds the axons of many neurons, especially those in the peripheral nervous system. The main consequence of a myelin sheath is an increase in the speed at which impulses propagate along the myelinated fiber. The sheath continues to develop throughout childhood.
Neuron	The neuron is the primary cell of the nervous system. They are found in the brain, the spinal cord, in the nerves and ganglia of the peripheral nervous system. It is a specialized cell that conducts impulses through the nervous system and contains three major parts: cell body, dendrites, and an axon. It can have many dendrites but only one axon.

Early adulthood	The developmental period beginning in the late teens or early twenties and lasting into the thirties is called early adulthood; characterized by an increasing self-awareness.
Synapse	A synapse is specialized junction through which cells of the nervous system signal to one another and to non-neuronal cells such as muscles or glands.
Late adolescence	Late adolescence refers to approximately the latter half of the second decade of life. Career interests, dating, and identity exploration are often more pronounced in late adolescence than in early adolescence.
Teratogen	Teratogen refers to from the Greek word tera, meaning 'monster.' It is any agent that causes a birth defect.
Fetus	A fetus develops from the end of the 8th week of pregnancy (when the major structures have formed), until birth.
Prostate	The prostate is a gland that supplies most of the fluid that makes up semen, it is located at the base of the uninary bladder.
Semen	Semen is a fluid that contains spermatozoa. It is secreted by the gonads of males for the fertilization of female ova.
Fallopian tube	A tube through which the eggs travel from the ovaries to the uterus is a fallopian tube.
Secondary sex characteristics	Secondary sex characteristics are traits that distinguish the two sexes of a species, but that are not directly part of the reproductive system.
Secondary sex characteristic	A secondary sex characteristic is a trait that distinguishes the two sexes of a species, but is not directly part of the reproductive system.
Penis	The penis is the external male copulatory organ and the external male organ of urination. In humans, the penis is homologous to the female clitoris, as it develops from the same embryonic structure. It is capable of erection for use in copulation.
Nocturnal	A person who exhibits nocturnal habits is referred to as a night owl.
Nocturnal emission	A nocturnal emission is an ejaculation of semen experienced by males during sleep. It is also called a "wet dream", an involuntary orgasm, or simply an orgasm during sleep.
Larynx	The larynx, or voicebox, is an organ in the neck of mammals involved in protection of the trachea and sound production. The larynx houses the vocal cords, and is situated at the point where the upper tract splits into the trachea and the esophagus.
Androgen	Androgen is the generic term for any natural or synthetic compound, usually a steroid hormone, that stimulates or controls the development and maintenance of masculine characteristics in vertebrates by binding to androgen receptors.
Uterus	The uterus or womb is the major female reproductive organ. The main function of the uterus is to accept a fertilized ovum which becomes implanted into the endometrium, and derives nourishment from blood vessels which develop exclusively for this purpose.
Seminal vesicles	The seminal vesicles are a pair of glands on the posterior surface of the urinary bladder of males. They secrete a significant proportion of the fluid that ultimately becomes semen.
Menarche	Menarche is the first menstrual period as a girl's body progresses through the changes of puberty. Menarche usually occurs about two years after the first changes of breast development.
Ovulation	Ovulation is the process in the menstrual cycle by which a mature ovarian follicle ruptures and discharges an ovum (also known as an oocyte, female gamete, or casually, an egg) that participates in reproduction.

Affect	A subjective feeling or emotional tone often accompanied by bodily expressions noticeable to others is called affect.
Twin study	A twin study is a kind of genetic study done to determine heritability. The premise is that since identical twins (especially identical twins raised apart) have identical genotypes, differences between them are solely due to environmental factors. By examining the degree to which twins are differentiated, a study may determine the extent to which a particular trait is influenced by genes or the environment.
Graham	Graham has conducted a number of studies that reveal stronger socioeconomic-status influences rather than ethnic influences in achievement.
Infancy	The developmental period that extends from birth to 18 or 24 months is called infancy.
Ejaculation	Ejaculation is the process of ejecting semen from the penis, and is usually accompanied by orgasm as a result of sexual stimulation.
Perception	Perception is the process of acquiring, interpreting, selecting, and organizing sensory information.
Attitude	An enduring mental representation of a person, place, or thing that evokes an emotional response and related behavior is called attitude.
Masturbation	Masturbation is the manual excitation of the sexual organs, most often to the point of orgasm. It can refer to excitation either by oneself or by another, but commonly refers to such activities performed alone.
Anxiety	Anxiety is a complex combination of the feeling of fear, apprehension and worry often accompanied by physical sensations such as palpitations, chest pain and/or shortness of breath.
Depression	In everyday language depression refers to any downturn in mood, which may be relatively transitory and perhaps due to something trivial. This is differentiated from Clinical depression which is marked by symptoms that last two weeks or more and are so severe that they interfere with daily living.
Ambivalence	The simultaneous holding of strong positive and negative emotional attitudes toward the same situation or person is called ambivalence.
Stereotype	A stereotype is considered to be a group concept, held by one social group about another. They are often used in a negative or prejudicial sense and are frequently used to justify certain discriminatory behaviors. This allows powerful social groups to legitimize and protect their dominant position
Eating disorders	Psychological disorders characterized by distortion of the body image and gross disturbances in eating patterns are called eating disorders.
Anorexia nervosa	Anorexia nervosa is an eating disorder characterized by voluntary starvation and exercise stress.
Attention	Attention is the cognitive process of selectively concentrating on one thing while ignoring other things. Psychologists have labeled three types of attention: sustained attention, selective attention, and divided attention.
Anorexia	Anorexia nervosa is an eating disorder characterized by voluntary starvation and exercise stress.
Malnutrition	Malnutrition is a general term for the medical condition in a person or animal caused by an unbalanced diet—either too little or too much food, or a diet missing one or more important nutrients.

Go to **Cram101.com** for the Practice Tests for this Chapter.

Bulimia	Bulimia refers to a disorder in which a person binges on incredibly large quantities of food, then purges by vomiting or by using laxatives. Bulimia is often less about food, and more to do with deep psychological issues and profound feelings of lack of control.
Binge	Binge refers to relatively brief episode of uncontrolled, excessive consumption.
Substance abuse	Substance abuse refers to the overindulgence in and dependence on a stimulant, depressant, or other chemical substance, leading to effects that are detrimental to the individual's physical or mental health, or the welfare of others.
Marijuana	Marijuana is the dried vegetable matter of the Cannabis sativa plant. It contains large concentrations of compounds that have medicinal and psychoactive effects when consumed, usually by smoking or eating.
Prospective study	Prospective study is a long-term study of a group of people, beginning before the onset of a common disorder. It allows investigators to see how the disorder develops.
Questionnaire	A self-report method of data collection or clinical assessment method in which the individual being studied checks off items on a printed list, answers multiple-choice questions, or writes out answers to essay questions aimed at producing a selfdescription is called questionnaire.
Obsession	An obsession is a thought or idea that the sufferer cannot stop thinking about. Common examples include fears of acquiring disease, getting hurt, or causing harm to someone. They are typically automatic, frequent, distressing, and difficult to control or put an end to by themselves.
Body image	A person's body image is their perception of their physical appearance. It is more than what a person thinks they will see in a mirror, it is inextricably tied to their self-esteem and acceptance by peers.
Chronic	Chronic refers to a relatively long duration, usually more than a few months.
Antidepressant	An antidepressant is a medication used primarily in the treatment of clinical depression. They are not thought to produce tolerance, although sudden withdrawal may produce adverse effects. They create little if any immediate change in mood and require between several days and several weeks to take effect.
Correlation	A statistical technique for determining the degree of association between two or more variables is referred to as correlation.
Psychological test	Psychological test refers to a standardized measure of a sample of a person's behavior.
Friendship	The essentials of friendship are reciprocity and commitment between individuals who see themselves more or less as equals. Interaction between friends rests on a more equal power base than the interaction between children and adults.
Clique	A clique is an informal and restricted social group formed by a number of people who share common. Social roles vary, but two roles commonly associated with a female clique is notably applicable to most - that of the "queen bee" and that of the "outcast".
Group structure	The network of roles, communication pathways, and power in a group is called the group structure.
Evolution	Commonly used to refer to gradual change, evolution is the change in the frequency of alleles within a population from one generation to the next. This change may be caused by different mechanisms, including natural selection, genetic drift, or changes in population (gene flow).
Autonomy	Autonomy is the condition of something that does not depend on anything else.

Norms	In testing, standards of test performance that permit the comparison of one person's score on the test to the scores of others who have taken the same test are referred to as norms.
Reciprocity	Reciprocity, in interpersonal attraction, is the tendency to return feelings and attitudes that are expressed about us.
Hartup	According to Hartup, the single best childhood predictor of adult adaptation is not school grades, and not classroom behavior, but rather, the adequacy with which the child gets along with other children.
Peer pressure	Peer pressure comprises a set of group dynamics whereby a group of people in which one feels comfortable may override the sexual personal habits, individual moral inhibitions or idiosyncratic desires to impose a group norm of attitudes or behaviors.
Gender difference	A gender difference is a disparity between genders involving quality or quantity. Though some gender differences are controversial, they are not to be confused with sexist stereotypes.
Homophobia	An intense, irrational hostility toward or fear of homosexuals is referred to as homophobia.
Homosexuality	Homosexuality refers to a sexual orientation characterized by aesthetic attraction, romantic love, and sexual desire exclusively for members of the same sex or gender identity.
Attachment	Attachment is the tendency to seek closeness to another person and feel secure when that person is present.
Eccles	Eccles was key to a number of important developments in neuroscience. Until around 1949, Eccles believed that synaptic transmission was primarily electrical rather than chemical. Although he was wrong in this hypothesis, his arguments led himself and others to perform some of the experiments which proved chemical synaptic transmission.
Syndrome	The term syndrome is the association of several clinically recognizable features, signs, symptoms, phenomena or characteristics which often occur together, so that the presence of one feature indicates the presence of the others.
Interdependence	Interdependence is a dynamic of being mutually responsible to and dependent on others.
Ethnic group	An ethnic group is a culture or subculture whose members are readily distinguishable by outsiders based on traits originating from a common racial, national, linguistic, or religious source. Members of an ethnic group are often presumed to be culturally or biologically similar, although this is not in fact necessarily the case.
Survey	A method of scientific investigation in which a large sample of people answer questions about their attitudes or behavior is referred to as a survey.
Socioeconomic	Socioeconomic pertains to the study of the social and economic impacts of any product or service offering, market intervention or other activity on an economy as a whole and on the companies, organization and individuals who are its main economic actors.
Ethnicity	Ethnicity refers to a characteristic based on cultural heritage, nationality characteristics, race, religion, and language.
Socioeconomic Status	A family's socioeconomic status is based on family income, parental education level, parental occupation, and social status in the community. Those with high status often have more success in preparing their children for school because they have access to a wide range of resources.
Anchor	An anchor is a sample of work or performance used to set the specific performance standard for a rubric level .
Population	Population refers to all members of a well-defined group of organisms, events, or things.
Construct	A generalized concept, such as anxiety or gravity, is a construct.

Go to **Cram101.com** for the Practice Tests for this Chapter.
And, **NEVER** highlight a book again!

Akers	Akers proposes that social behavior is shaped by a number of processes, including differential association, differential reinforcement, and cognitive definitions. He proposed that the same processes involved in learning and conforming behavior are involved in learning deviant behavior.
Socialization	Social rules and social relations are created, communicated, and changed in verbal and nonverbal ways creating social complexity useful in identifying outsiders and intelligent breeding partners. The process of learning these skills is called socialization.
Trait	An enduring personality characteristic that tends to lead to certain behaviors is called a trait. The term trait also means a genetically inherited feature of an organism.
Bronfenbrenner	Bronfenbrenner was a co-founder of the U.S. national Head Start program and founder of the Ecological Theory of Development.
Sexually Transmitted Disease	Sexually transmitted disease is commonly transmitted between partners through some form of sexual activity, most commonly vaginal intercourse, oral sex, or anal sex.
Learning	Learning is a relatively permanent change in behavior that results from experience. Thus, to attribute a behavioral change to learning, the change must be relatively permanent and must result from experience.
Sensation	Sensation is the first stage in the chain of biochemical and neurologic events that begins with the impinging of a stimulus upon the receptor cells of a sensory organ, which then leads to perception, the mental state that is reflected in statements like "I see a uniformly blue wall."
Sensation seeking	A generalized preference for high or low levels of sensory stimulation is referred to as sensation seeking.
Personality trait	According to the Diagnostic and Statistical Manual of the American Psychiatric Association, a personality trait is a "prominent aspect of personality that is exhibited in a wide range of important social and personal contexts. ...".
Hypothesis	A specific statement about behavior or mental processes that is testable through research is a hypothesis.
Exemplars	Exemplars refer to the individual instances of a concept that are stored in memory from personal experience.
Scientific research	Research that is objective, systematic, and testable is called scientific research.
Conformity	Conformity is the degree to which members of a group will change their behavior, views and attitudes to fit the views of the group. The group can influence members via unconscious processes or via overt social pressure on individuals.
Alcoholic	An alcoholic is dependent on alcohol as characterized by craving, loss of control, physical dependence and withdrawal symptoms, and tolerance.
Ethnographic study	Ethnographic study is an in-depth study of a culture, which uses a combination of methods including participant observation.
Statistics	Statistics is a type of data analysis which practice includes the planning, summarizing, and interpreting of observations of a system possibly followed by predicting or forecasting of future events based on a mathematical model of the system being observed.
Statistic	A statistic is an observable random variable of a sample.
Social class	Social class describes the relationships between people in hierarchical societies or

	cultures. Those with more power usually subordinate those with less power.
Infant mortality	Infant mortality is the death of infants in the first year of life. The leading causes of infant mortality are dehydration and disease. Major causes of infant mortality in more developed countries include congenital malformation, infection and SIDS. Infant mortality rate is the number of newborns dying under a year of age divided by the number of live births during the year.
Genitals	Genitals refers to the internal and external reproductive organs.
Script	A schema, or behavioral sequence, for an event is called a script. It is a form of schematic organization, with real-world events organized in terms of temporal and causal relations between component acts.
Variable	A variable refers to a measurable factor, characteristic, or attribute of an individual or a system.
Social Cohesion	Social Cohesion is a state in society where the vast majority of citizens respect the law and one another's human rights. To achieve Social Cohesion is one of the two functions of the law, the second fuction being to achieve social progress.
Lesbian	A lesbian is a homosexual woman. They are women who are sexually and romantically attracted to other women.
Arousal	Arousal is a physiological and psychological state involving the activation of the reticular activating system in the brain stem, the autonomic nervous system and the endocrine system, leading to increased heart rate and blood pressure and a condition of alertness and readiness to respond.
Clitoris	Clitoris refers to an external female sex organ that is highly sensitive to sexual stimulation.
Csikszentmihalyi	Csikszentmihalyi is noted for his work in the study of happiness, creativity, subjective well-being, and fun, but is best known for his having been the architect of the notion of flow: "... people are most happy when they are in a state of flow--a Zen-like state of total oneness...".
Personal space	Personal space is the region surrounding each person, or that area which a person considers his domain or territory. Often if entered by another being without this being desired, it makes them feel uncomfortable.
Domain Theory	Within domain theory a distinction is drawn between the child's developing concepts of morality, and other domains of social knowledge, such as social convention. According to domain theory, the child's concepts of morality and social convention emerge out of the child's attempts to account for qualitatively differing forms of social experience associated with these two classes of social events.
Obedience	Obedience is the willingness to follow the will of others. Humans have been shown to be surprisingly obedient in the presence of perceived legitimate authority figures, as demonstrated by the Milgram experiment in the 1960s.
Clinical study	An intensive investigation of a single person, especially one suffering from some injury or disease is referred to as a clinical study.
Problem solving	An attempt to find an appropriate way of attaining a goal when the goal is not readily available is called problem solving.
Social skills	Social skills are skills used to interact and communicate with others to assist status in the social structure and other motivations.
Stages	Stages represent relatively discrete periods of time in which functioning is qualitatively

194

195

	different from functioning at other periods.
Genital stage	The genital stage in psychology is the term used by Sigmund Freud to describe the final stage of human psychosexual development. It is characterized by the expression of libido through intercourse with an adult of the other gender.
Critical period	A period of time when an innate response can be elicited by a particular stimulus is referred to as the critical period.
Social identity	Social identity is the way we define ourselves in terms of group membership.
Physical attractiveness	Physical attractiveness is the perception of an individual as physically beautiful by other people.
Authoritative parents	Authoritative parents are strict and warm. Authoritative parents demand mature behavior but use reason rather than force in discipline.

Go to **Cram101.com** for the Practice Tests for this Chapter.

Go to **Cram101.com** for the Practice Tests for this Chapter.
And, **NEVER** highlight a book again!

Kohlberg	Kohlberg believed that people progressed in their moral reasoning through a series of developmental stages.
Reasoning	Reasoning is the act of using reason to derive a conclusion from certain premises. There are two main methods to reach a conclusion, deductive reasoning and inductive reasoning.
Clique	A clique is an informal and restricted social group formed by a number of people who share common. Social roles vary, but two roles commonly associated with a female clique is notably applicable to most - that of the "queen bee" and that of the "outcast".
Adolescence	The period of life bounded by puberty and the assumption of adult responsibilities is adolescence.
Wisdom	Wisdom is the ability to make correct judgments and decisions. It is an intangible quality gained through experience. Whether or not something is wise is determined in a pragmatic sense by its popularity, how long it has been around, and its ability to predict against future events.
Arnold Gesell	Arnold Gesell was a pioneer in the field of child development and developmental measurement. He constructed the Gesell dome, a one-way mirror shaped as a dome, under which children could be observed without being disturbed.
Role model	A person who serves as a positive example of desirable behavior is referred to as a role model.
Idealism	Idealism relates to direct knowledge of subjective mental ideas, or images. It is usually juxtaposed with realism in which the real is said to have absolute existence prior to and independent of our knowledge.
Piaget	Piaget argued that young children's answers were qualitatively different than older children rather than quantitative. There are two major aspects to his theory: the process of coming to know and the stages we move through as we gradually acquire this ability.
Formal operational	According to Piaget, the period from age 12 to adulthood, which is characterized by abstract thought is referred to as the formal operational stage.
Cognitive development	The process by which a child's understanding of the world changes as a function of age and experience is called cognitive development.
Cognition	The intellectual processes through which information is obtained, transformed, stored, retrieved, and otherwise used is cognition.
Personal identity	The portion of the self-concept that pertains to the self as a distinct, separate individual is called personal identity.
Concrete operational	According to Piaget, the period from 7 to 12 years of age, which is characterized by logical thought and a loss of egocentrism, is referred to as concrete operational stage. Conservation skills are formed - understanding that quantity, length or number of items is unrelated to the appearance of the object or items.
Abstract principles	Concepts and ideas isolated from specific examples and concrete situations are referrd to as abstract principles.
Universal ethical principles	In Kohlberg's sixth stage, universal ethical principles, moral reasoning is based on the use of abstract reasoning using universal ethical principles.
Hypocrisy	Publicly advocating some attitude or behavior and then acting in a way that is inconsistent with this espoused attitude or behavior is called hypocrisy.
Variable	A variable refers to a measurable factor, characteristic, or attribute of an individual or a

Go to **Cram101.com** for the Practice Tests for this Chapter.

	system.
Inhelder and Piaget	Inhelder and Piaget (1958) "...the maturation of the nervous system can do no more than determine the totality of possibilities and impossibilities at a given stage."
Formal operations	Formal operations in Piaget's theory is the final stage of cognitive development, in which children are able to apply abstract logical rules. Not everyone reaches the formal operations stage of development.
Construct	A generalized concept, such as anxiety or gravity, is a construct.
Rationalism	Rationalism is a philosophical doctrine that asserts that the truth should be determined by reason and factual analysis, rather than faith, dogma or religious teaching. Rationalism has some similarities in ideology and intent to humanism and atheism, in that it aims to provide a framework for social and philosophical discourse outside of religious or supernatural beliefs.
Premise	A premise is a statement presumed true within the context of a discourse, especially of a logical argument.
Deductive reasoning	Deductive reasoning refers to a form of reasoning about arguments in which conclusions are determined from the premises. The conclusions are true if the premises are true.
Assimilation	According to Piaget, assimilation is the process of the organism interacting with the environment given the organism's cognitive structure. Assimilation is reuse of schemas to fit new information.
Equilibration	Equilibration is a mechanism in Piaget's theory that explains how children or adolescents shift from one state of thought to the next. The shift occurs as they experience cognitive conflict or disequilibrium in trying to understand the world. It is an innate drive to organize experiences to ensure maximal adaptation.
Insight	Insight refers to a sudden awareness of the relationships among various elements that had previously appeared to be independent of one another.
Knowledge base	The general background information a person possesses, which influences most cognitive task performance is called the knowledge base.
Problem solving	An attempt to find an appropriate way of attaining a goal when the goal is not readily available is called problem solving.
Working Memory	Working memory is the collection of structures and processes in the brain used for temporarily storing and manipulating information. Working memory consists of both memory for items that are currently being processed, and components governing attention and directing the processing itself.
Acquisition	Acquisition is the process of adapting to the environment, learning or becoming conditioned. In classical conditoning terms, it is the initial learning of the stimulus response link, which involves a neutral stimulus being associated with a unconditioned stimulus and becoming a conditioned stimulus.
Reliability	Reliability means the extent to which a test produces a consistent , reproducible score .
Qualitative change	A qualitative change refers to a change in kind, structure, or organization, such as the change from nonverbal to verbal communication.
Social policy	Social policy is the study of the welfare state, and the range of responses to social need.
Variability	Statistically, variability refers to how much the scores in a distribution spread out, away from the mean.
Intuition	Quick, impulsive thought that does not make use of formal logic or clear reasoning is

referred to as intuition.

Scientific reasoning	A type of reasoning that involves the generation of hypotheses and the systematic testing of those hypotheses is scientific reasoning.
Script	A schema, or behavioral sequence, for an event is called a script. It is a form of schematic organization, with real-world events organized in terms of temporal and causal relations between component acts.
Formal reasoning	The type of reasoning in which the form of an argument, not its semantic content, is crucial is referred to as formal reasoning.
Gender difference	A gender difference is a disparity between genders involving quality or quantity. Though some gender differences are controversial, they are not to be confused with sexist stereotypes.
Stages	Stages represent relatively discrete periods of time in which functioning is qualitatively different from functioning at other periods.
Population	Population refers to all members of a well-defined group of organisms, events, or things.
Society	The social sciences use the term society to mean a group of people that form a semi-closed (or semi-open) social system, in which most interactions are with other individuals belonging to the group.
Moral reasoning	Moral reasoning involves concepts of justice, whereas social conventional judgments are concepts of social organization.
Preconventional level	According to Kohlberg, the preconventional level is a period during which moral judgments are based largely on expectation of rewards or punishments.
Conventional level	According to Kohlberg, a period during which moral judgments is largely reflective of social conventions is the conventional level. It is a "law and order" approach to morality.
Punishment	Punishment is the addtion of a stimulus that reduces the frequency of a response, or the removal of a stimulus that results in a reduction of the response.
Obedience	Obedience is the willingness to follow the will of others. Humans have been shown to be surprisingly obedient in the presence of perceived legitimate authority figures, as demonstrated by the Milgram experiment in the 1960s.
Individualistic	Cultures have been classified as individualistic, which means having a set of values that give priority to personal goals rather than group goals.
Friendship	The essentials of friendship are reciprocity and commitment between individuals who see themselves more or less as equals. Interaction between friends rests on a more equal power base than the interaction between children and adults.
Validity	The extent to which a test measures what it is intended to measure is called validity.
Attachment	Attachment is the tendency to seek closeness to another person and feel secure when that person is present.
Moral judgment	Making decisions about which actions are right and which are wrong is a moral judgment.
Early adulthood	The developmental period beginning in the late teens or early twenties and lasting into the thirties is called early adulthood; characterized by an increasing self-awareness.
Morality of Care	By listening to women's experiences, Gilligan offered that a morality of care can serve in the place of the morality of justice and rights espoused by Kohlberg. In her view, the morality of caring and responsibility is premised in nonviolence, while the morality of justice and rights is based on equality.
Carol Gilligan	Carol Gilligan is best known for her work on the ethics of care, a theory that contrasts

ethics of care to so-called ethics of justice. She claimed that the results of Kohlberg were biased because the participants in the basic study were largely male, and that the scoring method subsequently used tended to favor a principled way of reasoning that was more common to boys, over a moral argumentation concentrating on relations, which would be more amenable to girls.

Stereotype	A stereotype is considered to be a group concept, held by one social group about another. They are often used in a negative or prejudicial sense and are frequently used to justify certain discriminatory behaviors. This allows powerful social groups to legitimize and protect their dominant position
Anecdotal evidence	Anecdotal evidence is unreliable evidence based on personal experience that has not been empirically tested, and which is often used in an argument as if it had been scientifically or statistically proven. The person using anecdotal evidence may or may not be aware of the fact that, by doing so, they are generalizing.
Moral development	Development regarding rules and conventions about what people should do in their interactions with other people is called moral development.
Bias	A bias is a prejudice in a general or specific sense, usually in the sense for having a preference to one particular point of view or ideological perspective.
Social role	Social role refers to expected behavior patterns associated with particular social positions.
Norms	In testing, standards of test performance that permit the comparison of one person's score on the test to the scores of others who have taken the same test are referred to as norms.
Ambivalence	The simultaneous holding of strong positive and negative emotional attitudes toward the same situation or person is called ambivalence.
Correlation	A statistical technique for determining the degree of association between two or more variables is referred to as correlation.
Attitude	An enduring mental representation of a person, place, or thing that evokes an emotional response and related behavior is called attitude.
Personality	Personality refers to the pattern of enduring characteristics that differentiates a person, the patterns of behaviors that make each individual unique.
Erik Erikson	Erik Erikson conceived eight stages of development, each confronting the individual with its own psychosocial demands, that continued into old age. Personality development, according to Erikson, takes place through a series of crises that must be overcome and internalized by the individual in preparation for the next developmental stage. Such crisis are not catastrophes but vulnerabilities.
William James	Functionalism as a psychology developed out of Pragmatism as a philosophy: To find the meaning of an idea, you have to look at its consequences. This led William James and his students towards an emphasis on cause and effect, prediction and control, and observation of environment and behavior, over the careful introspection of the Structuralists.
Reflection	Reflection is the process of rephrasing or repeating thoughts and feelings expressed, making the person more aware of what they are saying or thinking.
Emotion	An emotion is a mental states that arise spontaneously, rather than through conscious effort. They are often accompanied by physiological changes.
Quantitative	A quantitative property is one that exists in a range of magnitudes, and can therefore be measured. Measurements of any particular quantitative property are expressed as as a specific quantity, referred to as a unit, multiplied by a number.
Marcia	Marcia argued that identity could be viewed as a structure of beliefs, abilities and past

experiences regarding the self. Identity is a dynamic, not static structure. At least three aspects of the adolescent's development are important in identity formation: must be confident that they have parental support, must have an established sense of industry, and must be able to adopt a self-reflective stance toward the future.

Identity crisis	Erikson coinded the term identity crisis: "...a psychosocial state or condition of disorientation and role confusion occurring especially in adolescents as a result of conflicting internal and external experiences, pressures, and expectations and often producing acute anxiety."
Identity Achievement	Identity achievement is Marcia's term for an adolescent's having undergone a crisis and made a commitment.
Identity diffusion	Identity diffusion is Marcia's term for adolescents who have not yet experienced a crisis or made any commitments.
Darwin	Darwin achieved lasting fame as originator of the theory of evolution through natural selection. His book Expression of Emotions in Man and Animals is generally considered the first text on comparative psychology.
Evolution	Commonly used to refer to gradual change, evolution is the change in the frequency of alleles within a population from one generation to the next. This change may be caused by different mechanisms, including natural selection, genetic drift, or changes in population (gene flow).
Species	Species refers to a reproductively isolated breeding population.
Motives	Needs or desires that energize and direct behavior toward a goal are motives.
Puberty	Puberty refers to the process of physical changes by which a child's body becomes an adult body capable of reproduction.
Autonomy	Autonomy is the condition of something that does not depend on anything else.
Sympathetic	The sympathetic nervous system activates what is often termed the "fight or flight response". It is an automatic regulation system, that is, one that operates without the intervention of conscious thought.
Shaping	The concept of reinforcing successive, increasingly accurate approximations to a target behavior is called shaping. The target behavior is broken down into a hierarchy of elemental steps, each step more sophisticated then the last. By successively reinforcing each of the the elemental steps, a form of differential reinforcement, until that step is learned while extinguishing the step below, the target behavior is gradually achieved.
Counselor	A counselor is a mental health professional who specializes in helping people with problems not involving serious mental disorders.
Sigmund Freud	Sigmund Freud was the founder of the psychoanalytic school, based on his theory that unconscious motives control much behavior, that particular kinds of unconscious thoughts and memories are the source of neurosis, and that neurosis could be treated through bringing these unconscious thoughts and memories to consciousness in psychoanalytic treatment.
Infancy	The developmental period that extends from birth to 18 or 24 months is called infancy.
Repression	A defense mechanism, repression involves moving thoughts unacceptable to the ego into the unconscious, where they cannot be easily accessed.
Incest	Incest refers to sexual relations between close relatives, most often between daughter and father or between brother and sister.
Sexism	Sexism is commonly considered to be discrimination against people based on their sex rather than their individual merits, but can also refer to any and all differentiations based on

Perception	Perception is the process of acquiring, interpreting, selecting, and organizing sensory information.
Sexual orientation	Sexual orientation refers to the sex or gender of people who are the focus of a person's amorous or erotic desires, fantasies, and spontaneous feelings, the gender(s) toward which one is primarily "oriented".
Lesbian	A lesbian is a homosexual woman. They are women who are sexually and romantically attracted to other women.
Representative sample	Representative sample refers to a sample of participants selected from the larger population in such a way that important subgroups within the population are included in the sample in the same proportions as they are found in the larger population.
Sensitization	Sensitization is a process whereby an organism is made more responsive to certain aspects of its environment. For example, increases in the effects of a drug as a result of repeated administration. Also known as reverse tolerance.
Homosexual	Homosexual refers to a sexual orientation characterized by aesthetic attraction, romantic love, and sexual desire exclusively for members of the same sex or gender identity.
Late adolescence	Late adolescence refers to approximately the latter half of the second decade of life. Career interests, dating, and identity exploration are often more pronounced in late adolescence than in early adolescence.
Homosexuality	Homosexuality refers to a sexual orientation characterized by aesthetic attraction, romantic love, and sexual desire exclusively for members of the same sex or gender identity.
Learning	Learning is a relatively permanent change in behavior that results from experience. Thus, to attribute a behavioral change to learning, the change must be relatively permanent and must result from experience.
Ethnic identity	An enduring, basic aspect of the self that includes a sense of membership in an ethnic group and the attitudes and feelings related to that membership is called an ethnic identity.
Cultural values	The importance and desirability of various objects and activities as defined by people in a given culture are referred to as cultural values.
Ethnic group	An ethnic group is a culture or subculture whose members are readily distinguishable by outsiders based on traits originating from a common racial, national, linguistic, or religious source. Members of an ethnic group are often presumed to be culturally or biologically similar, although this is not in fact necessarily the case.
Suicide	Suicide behavior is rare in childhood but escalates in adolescence. The suicide rate increases in a linear fashion from adolescence through late adulthood.
Normative	The term normative is used to describe the effects of those structures of culture which regulate the function of social activity.
Psychological disorder	Mental processes and/or behavior patterns that cause emotional distress and/or substantial impairment in functioning is a psychological disorder.
Ethnicity	Ethnicity refers to a characteristic based on cultural heritage, nationality characteristics, race, religion, and language.
Ethnographic study	Ethnographic study is an in-depth study of a culture, which uses a combination of methods including participant observation.
Anchor	An anchor is a sample of work or performance used to set the specific performance standard for a rubric level .
Collectivist	A person who defines the self in terms of relationships to other people and groups and gives

priority to group goals is called collectivist.

Interdependence	Interdependence is a dynamic of being mutually responsible to and dependent on others.
Statistic	A statistic is an observable random variable of a sample.
Bruner	Bruner has had an enormous impact on educational psychology with his contributions to cognitive learning theory. His ideas are based on categorization, maintaining that people interpret the world in terms of its similarities and differences.
Rite of passage	A rite of passage is a ritual that marks a change in a person's social or sexual status. The term was popularized by the French ethnographer Arnold van Gennep (1873-1957), in the early part of the twentieth century.
Individualist	A person who defines the self in terms of personal traits and gives priority to personal goals is an individualist.
Prejudice	Prejudice in general, implies coming to a judgment on the subject before learning where the preponderance of the evidence actually lies, or formation of a judgement without direct experience.
Rites of passage	Rites of passage are rituals that marks a change in a person's social or sexual status. The term was popularized by the French ethnographer Arnold van Gennep (1873-1957), in the early part of the twentieth century.
Attention	Attention is the cognitive process of selectively concentrating on one thing while ignoring other things. Psychologists have labeled three types of attention: sustained attention, selective attention, and divided attention.
Subculture	As understood in sociology, anthropology and cultural studies, a subculture is a set of people with a distinct set of behavior and beliefs that differentiate them from a larger culture of which they are a part.
Nurture	Nurture refers to the environmental influences on behavior due to nutrition, culture, socioeconomic status, and learning.
Affect	A subjective feeling or emotional tone often accompanied by bodily expressions noticeable to others is called affect.
Causation	Causation concerns the time order relationship between two or more objects such that if a specific antecendent condition occurs the same consequent must always follow.
Ideology	An ideology can be thought of as a comprehensive vision, as a way of looking at things, as in common sense and several philosophical tendencies, or a set of ideas proposed by the dominant class of a society to all members of this society.
Bronfenbrenner	Bronfenbrenner was a co-founder of the U.S. national Head Start program and founder of the Ecological Theory of Development.
Theories	Theories are logically self-consistent models or frameworks describing the behavior of a certain natural or social phenomenon. They are broad explanations and predictions concerning phenomena of interest.
Ecological perspective	The view that different learning mechanisms have developed through natural selection to serve different survival needs and that these mechanisms are best understood in relation to life in the natural environment is referred to as the ecological perspective.
Substance abuse	Substance abuse refers to the overindulgence in and dependence on a stimulant, depressant, or other chemical substance, leading to effects that are detrimental to the individual's physical or mental health, or the welfare of others.
Eccles	Eccles was key to a number of important developments in neuroscience. Until around 1949,

210

	Eccles believed that synaptic transmission was primarily electrical rather than chemical. Although he was wrong in this hypothesis, his arguments led himself and others to perform some of the experiments which proved chemical synaptic transmission.
Postconventi-nal reasoning	Postconventional reasoning is the highest level in Kohlberg's theory of moral development. Morality is completely internalized. These individuals reason based on the principles which underlie rules and norms, but reject a uniform application of a rule or norm.
Developmental psychologist	A psychologist interested in human growth and development from conception until death is referred to as a developmental psychologist.
Oedipus complex	The Oedipus complex is a concept developed by Sigmund Freud to explain the maturation of the infant boy through identification with the father and desire for the mother.
Prenatal	Prenatal period refers to the time from conception to birth.
Heredity	Heredity is the transfer of characteristics from parent to offspring through their genes.
Androgen	Androgen is the generic term for any natural or synthetic compound, usually a steroid hormone, that stimulates or controls the development and maintenance of masculine characteristics in vertebrates by binding to androgen receptors.
Feedback	Feedback refers to information returned to a person about the effects a response has had.
Testosterone	Testosterone is a steroid hormone from the androgen group. It is the principal male sex hormone and the "original" anabolic steroid.
Gonads	The gonads are the organs that make gametes. Gametes are haploid germ cells. For example, sperm and egg cells are gametes. In the male the gonads are the testicles, and in the female the gonads are the ovaries.
Embryo	A developed zygote that has a rudimentary heart, brain, and other organs is referred to as an embryo.
Nerve	A nerve is an enclosed, cable-like bundle of nerve fibers or axons, which includes the glia that ensheath the axons in myelin. Neurons are sometimes called nerve cells, though this term is technically imprecise since many neurons do not form nerves.
Primary emotions	Primary emotions, according to Robert Plutchik's theory, are the most basic emotions which include fear, surprise, sadness, disgust, anger, anticipation, joy, and acceptance. Each has high survival value.
Socialization	Social rules and social relations are created, communicated, and changed in verbal and nonverbal ways creating social complexity useful in identifying outsiders and intelligent breeding partners. The process of learning these skills is called socialization.
Thalidomide	Thalidomide is a drug which was sold during the 1950s and 1960s as a sleeping aid and to pregnant women as an antiemetic to combat morning sickness and other symptoms. It was later (1960–61) found to be teratogenic in fetal development, most visibly as a cause of amelia or phocomelia.
Cultural diversity	Cultural diversity is the variety of human societies or cultures in a specific region, or in the world as a whole.
Brain	The brain controls and coordinates most movement, behavior and homeostatic body functions such as heartbeat, blood pressure, fluid balance and body temperature. Functions of the brain are responsible for cognition, emotion, memory, motor learning and other sorts of learning. The brain is primarily made up of two types of cells: glia and neurons.
Sensorimotor	The first of Piaget's stages is the Sensorimotor stage. This stage typically ranges from birth to 2 years. In this stage, children experience the world through their senses. During

this stage, object permanence and stranger anxiety develop.

Deprivation	Deprivation, is the loss or withholding of normal stimulation, nutrition, comfort, love, and so forth; a condition of lacking. The level of stimulation is less than what is required.
Social influence	Social influence is when the actions or thoughts of individual(s) are changed by other individual(s). Peer pressure is an example of social influence.
Internalization	The developmental change from behavior that is externally controlled to behavior that is controlled by internal standards and principles is referred to as internalization.
Temperament	Temperament refers to a basic, innate disposition to change behavior. The activity level is an important dimension of temperament.
Maturation	The orderly unfolding of traits, as regulated by the genetic code is called maturation.
Empathy	Empathy is the recognition and understanding of the states of mind, including beliefs, desires and particularly emotions of others without injecting your own.

Printed in the United Kingdom
by Lightning Source UK Ltd.
120640UK00001B/77-86